COMPLETE POEMS 1941/1994

SANGHARAKSHITA

complete poems

1941/1994

WINDHORSE

Published by Windhorse Publications
Unit 1-316 The Custard Factory
Gibb Street
Birmingham
B9 4AA

© Sangharakshita 1995

Printed by Redwood Books,
Trowbridge, Wiltshire

Cover illustration   Chintamani
Design   Dhammarati

British Library Cataloguing in Publication Data
A catalogue record for this book is available from the British Library

ISBN 0 904766 70 5

Also by Sangharakshita

A Survey of Buddhism
Flame in Darkness
The Three Jewels
Crossing the Stream
The Essence of Zen
The Thousand-Petalled Lotus
Human Enlightenment
The Religion of Art
The Ten Pillars of Buddhism
The Eternal Legacy
Travel Letters
Alternative Traditions
Ambedkar and Buddhism
The History of My Going for Refuge
The Taste of Freedom
New Currents in Western Buddhism
A Guide to the Buddhist Path
Learning to Walk
Vision and Transformation
The Buddha's Victory
Facing Mount Kanchenjunga
The FWBO and 'Protestant Buddhism'
The Drama of Cosmic Enlightenment
Wisdom Beyond Words
The Priceless Jewel
Who is the Buddha?
The Meaning of Orthodoxy in Buddhism
Mind Reactive and Creative
Going For Refuge
My Relation to the Order
Buddhism and the West
Forty-Three Years Ago
The Meaning of Conversion in Buddhism
Was the Buddha a Bhikkhu?
In the Realm of the Lotus
Peace is a Fire
The Inconceivable Emancipation

A SHORT BIOGRAPHY OF SANGHARAKSHITA

SANGHARAKSHITA'S FIRST remembered contact with Buddhism is of being held up as a child to inspect a large painting of a Buddha hanging in his grandmother's front hall.

Born Dennis Lingwood in Stockwell, London, in 1925, his first opportunity to explore the cultural riches of the world came early, when a suspected heart condition confined him to bed between the ages of eight and ten. Initiated into the culture of East and West by Harmsworth's *Children's Encyclopaedia*, he went on to pursue a passion for art, literature, and history with great precocity.

After being profoundly affected by Milton's *Paradise Lost*, thirteen-year-old Dennis began an epic of his own, his first poem. At sixteen he discovered through reading the classics of the East that he was a Buddhist. When army life took him to India, he devoted himself as much as possible to the study and practice of the Buddha's teachings.

Staying in India after leaving the Army, he was ordained as a monk, and given the name Sangharakshita, which means 'protector of the spiritual community'. It was around this time that he began to experience a tension between his spiritual and his artistic vision which provoked much reflection on the relationship between the Arts and Buddhism. The sage and the poet were soon united however, as it became clear that the two aspects were complementary, both having the same aspiration to higher human development.

During the fourteen years he spent in Kalimpong, Sangharakshita continued to read and write prodigiously, his poetry being often inspired by the majestic mountains facing his vihara, and by his reflections on the transformative effect of beauty, a theme that runs through much of his writing.

Meanwhile, there was a rising interest in Buddhism in the West, but a lack of vitality and vision. Aware that his experience might help in leading a new way forward, Sangharakshita returned to England in 1964 and soon founded a new movement called the Friends of the Western Buddhist Order.

From the earliest days of the FWBO's foundation, Sangharakshita has consistently encouraged the poets, painters, and other artists among his disciples, and highlighted the importance of engaging with Western culture and art. He has evolved a body of teachings showing that the inclusion of the Arts in the spiritual life can help the developing individual to achieve a harmonious integration of reason and emotion.

Almost thirty years after founding the FWBO, Sangharakshita is handing on to his senior disciples most of his responsibilities for running the movement. He now wants to focus on personal contact with people, and of course, on his writing. Having expressed himself poetically throughout his life, his poetry, collected here for the first time, constitutes a unique insight into this remarkable man and his extraordinary journey.

Lottie Berthoud
Norwich
10 May 1995

... I stayed alone
Thinking over every tone
Which, though silent to the ear,
The enchanted heart could hear.
SHELLEY

PREFACE

I HAVE WRITTEN poetry since I was eleven or twelve. Throughout my teens and well into my twenties, I wrote an enormous quantity of it, most of which has not survived. The poems appearing in this collection are selected from my published and unpublished output during the years 1941–1994, and represent all I would wish to preserve. Not that they are all necessarily worth preserving as poetry. Many of them, if not the majority, have only a biographical – even a sentimental – interest. They give expression to passing moods and fancies as well as to deeper experiences and insights. They also reflect my response to my surroundings. As such they constitute a sort of spiritual autobiography, sketchy indeed, but perhaps revealing, or at least suggesting, aspects of my life that would not otherwise be known. Some of my friends, I believe, may find an autobiography of this sort of greater interest than a more formal account. They may also enjoy, as poetry, those few poems which may be considered to rank as such. For the sake of these friends – old and new, Eastern and Western – I am bringing out this collection, and to them I affectionately dedicate it.

Sangharakshita
London
27 February 1995

CONTENTS

   3 A Short Biography of Sangharakshita
   7 Preface

PART I SHORTER POEMS

23 London in Wartime
24 Systole and Diastole
26 The Taoist Teacher
27 'Water From the Thawed-Out Snow…'
28 To a Political Friend
29 To Chenrezi
30 Lines
31 Meditation
32 The Wheel of Dharma
33 Music at Night
34 The Wandering Singer
36 The Clouded Dragon
38 Before an Image of the Buddha
40 The Moon of Beauty
41 Night Thoughts
43 Rain
44 The Parable of the Plough
46 'Above Me Broods…'

47	Aspiration
48	Himalayan Sages
49	The Four Sights
53	Sonnet
54	Wesak Joy
55	The Sun-Path
57	Advent
58	Secret Wings
59	The Tramp
61	Sri Pada
62	The Poet's Reply
63	'Tired of the Crimson Curtain…'
65	Peace
66	The Word of the Buddha
67	Wesak Thoughts
72	To the Recumbent Buddha
74	The Wounded Swan
77	The Face of Silence
79	The Lord of Compassion
80	Truth, Love, Life and Man
81	The Message of the Bowl
84	The Citadel
85	The White Calf
87	Tendai
88	The Lotus of Compassion
89	The Only Way
90	The Birthplace of Compassion
91	The Fragrance of Compassion
92	On the Brink
93	Invocation
94	The Alms of Compassion
95	The Unseen Flower

96	Village India
98	Rhymed Tanka
98	Rhymed Haiku
99	The Lamp of Compassion
100	Mountains
101	Messengers from Tibet
103	Bamboos
104	Stanzas
105	The Gardener
106	Kanchenjunga
106	Rhymed Haiku
107	The Bodhisattva
108	'White Mist Drifts Down the Valley Dim…'
109	Life's Furnace
110	Inaccessible
111	Frustration
112	Transience
113	'The Ashes of all my Heartaches…'
114	Love's Austerity
115	'It is not Love that Seeks to Bind…'
116	The Evening Walk
117	Goldfish
118	Bamboo Orchids
119	Yashodhara
120	Quatrain
121	The Secret
122	'Many Were The Friends…'
124	Longing
125	The Root Speaks
126	'Forgive Me if I Have Stained…'
127	The Heart's No
128	Lines

129	Maitreya
130	Plato's Reply
131	Song
132	Rhymed Haiku
132	Rhymed Haiku
132	Rhymed Haiku
133	Rhymed Haiku
133	Rhymed Haiku
134	Lumbini
135	Animist
136	The Poet's Eye
137	The Charcoal-Burners
139	Buffaloes Being Driven to Market
141	No Word
142	Quatrain
143	'Up and Down the Gravel Path…'
144	Tibetan Trumpets
145	Hieroglyphics
146	'I Think There Lives More Wisdom…'
147	Man's Way
148	'In the Woods are Many More'
149	Summer Afternoon
150	Awakening
151	Haiku
151	Haiku
152	Lines
153	Manifesto
154	The Survivor
155	A Rainy Day in the Mountains
157	The Abominable Snowman
159	Reciprocity
160	Transformation

161	Taking Refuge in the Buddha
164	Looking at the Moon on a Frosty Night
165	Winter in the Hills
166	Argosies
167	The Tree of Wisdom
170	Certainties
171	The Modern Bard
172	Madrigal
173	The Pioneer
174	The Conquest of Mara
175	Epitaph on Krishna, Princess Irene's Squirrel
176	Sonnet
177	Sonnet
178	The Bodhisattva's Reply
180	Immensities
181	On a Political Procession
182	Calcutta
183	Nagarjunikonda
185	The Vase of Moonlight
186	The Stream of Stars
187	Nocturne
188	Joy in Flight
189	The Great Work
190	Lines
191	Elusive Beauty
193	Epigram
194	A Crumb From the Symposium
195	Stanzas
196	Kalinga
197	Defiance
198	The Quest
199	Sonnet

200	Quatrain
200	Rhymed Haiku
201	Possibilities
202	Nalanda Revisited
203	To Manjushri
204	Hope
205	The Voice of Silence
206	Memory
207	Quatrain
208	Sonnet
209	Quatrain
210	Sonnet
211	Sonnet
212	The Cult of the Young Hero
213	Life and Death
214	Stanzas
215	A Life
216	Triolet
217	Quatrain
217	Quatrain
218	Stanzas
219	Couplet
220	Spring – Winter
221	Study in Blue and White
222	Lepcha Song
223	Stanzas
224	Quatrains
225	Sappho
226	'My Soul Between the Feeling and the Thought…'
227	Visiting the Taj Mahal at the Time of the Suez Canal Crisis and Seeing the Tombs of the Emperor Shah Jahan and Mumtaz Mahal

228	The Sangha
229	The Scholars
230	Quatrain
230	Quatrain
231	To ——
232	Quatrain
232	Epitaph on a 'Poem'
233	Stanzas
234	Couplet Haiku
234	Lines
235	Return Journey
236	Meditation on a Flame
237	In Praise of Water
238	The Young Hills
239	The Guardian Wall
240	Rhymed Haiku
240	Haiku
240	Quatrain
241	Siddhartha's Dream
242	The Three Marks
243	Three Couplet Haikus
244	The Buddha
245	Tibetan Refugee
246	Points of View
247	To Shrimati Sophia Wadia in Honour of her Sixtieth Birthday
250	Spring
251	Planting the Bodhi Tree
252	Waiting in the Car
253	Couplet Haiku
254	Stanzas
255	Poems for Four Friends

256	Ten Vignettes
258	The Crystal Rosary
259	After Meditation
260	Chinese Poems
264	'I Want to Break Out…'
265	'From the Ever-Faithful Present…'
266	The Mask
267	The Martyrdom of Saint Sebastian
268	Orpheus in the Underworld
269	St Jerome in the Desert
270	For the Record
272	New
274	Petals
276	Haiku
276	Wish
277	Fourth Metamorphosis
278	Variations on a Mersey Sound I
280	Variation on a Mersey Sound II
282	Mother
283	The Time Has Come…
284	Dream
285	Life is King
286	Mirrors
287	Scapegoat
289	At the Barber's
290	In the New Forest
291	Criminals
292	Sangharakshita's Verses of Acknowledgement
294	Easter Retreat
295	Sequence in a Strange Land
298	The Ballad of Journeyman Death
299	Four Gifts

300	Homage to William Blake
301	Song of the Windhorse
304	May
305	I.M., J. and K.
306	Autumn Vignette
307	The Gods
308	Padmaloka
310	The Sunflower's Farewell
311	The Priest's Dream
312	Before Dawn
313	Lines Written for the Dedication of the Shrine and the Opening of the London Buddhist Centre
314	Too Late
315	The Sirens
316	Alexandrines Perhaps
317	After Reading the Vimalakirti-Nirdesha
318	Hope
319	Verses
320	Sonnet
321	The Scapegoat
322	Resurrection
323	Haiku
324	Greenstone
325	Epigram
326	Lovelace Revisited
327	Snow-White Revisited
328	The Realms of Existence as Depicted in the Tibetan Wheel of Life
332	After Rilke
333	The Stricken Giant
334	'Blake Walked Among the Stones of Fire…'
335	The Dream

336	Lines Composed on Retreat During a Period of Silence
337	Epigram on Molly the Medium
338	Yemen Revisited
339	A Wish
340	Lines to Jayapushpa on Her Return to Malaysia
341	Tuscany 1983
342	St Francis and the Birds
344	Three Rubáiyát
345	Lines Composed on Acquiring 'The Works of Samuel Johnson, LL.D.', in Eleven Volumes, MDCCLXXXVII
349	The Wondering Heart
351	Bhájá, 1983
352	Poems on Paintings From the 'Genius of Venice' Exhibition at the Royal Academy
358	Minerva's Rebuke to Jean Cocteau
359	Three Epitaphs
360	The Golden Flower
361	The Ballad of the Return Journey
362	I.M., Tarashri
363	The People of Bethnal Green
364	The Oak and the Ivy
365	Paradise Lost
366	Betrayal
367	'A Man was Walking Behind Me…'
368	'The Past is in the Mind…'
369	The Great Things of Guhyaloka
371	An Old Story
372	Time and Eternity
373	Birds and Their Gods
377	Muchalinda
379	Diptych

380	For P—— on Solitary Retreat
382	The Gods
383	Work and Play
384	Contraries
385	The Neoplatonists
386	People Like Things Labelled
387	Yesterday's Blossoms
387	Crystal Ball
387	My Life
388	The Teacher of Gods and Men
389	Four Haiku
390	To P—— in Prague
391	Zen
392	London Bridge
393	On a Certain Author
393	Remembering the Poetry Reading
394	'Surely King Mark was Mad…'
395	The Poetry of Friendship

PART 2   LONGER POEMS

401	The Awakening of the Heart
417	The Veil of Stars
439	On Glastonbury Tor
449	The Caves of Bhájá
459	Hercules and the Birds

PART 3   TRANSLATIONS

Translations from the Pali

473	Auspicious Signs
475	Loving Kindness

477 Jewels
481 Outside the Walls
483 The Buried Treasure
485 Salutation to the Three Jewels

Translations from the Tibetan
489 Invocation to the Wrathful Deities
491 Offering the Mandala

APPENDIX I

493 Introduction to 'The Veil of Stars'

APPENDIX II

501 Argument Prefixed to 'The Veil of Stars'

505 NOTES

509 INDEX OF FIRST LINES

Note: An asterisk after the title of a poem indicates that there is a note at the end of the book, the note referring either to the poem as a whole or to some special passage in it.

part I shorter poems

LONDON IN WARTIME 1941

Athens, the olive and grey eyes,
And Rome, the martyred whore;
Paris, Berlin and Amsterdam,
Madrid, a hundred more:

This city makes their glories fade,
Her splendour makes them dumb –
London, on whose majestic brow
All the ends of the world are come.

1946 SYSTOLE AND DIASTOLE*

Whén the latency of thought
   Has winged itself with power to be
And flashes from its former naught
   Into actuality,
The consciousness of man expands like light,
Conquering new worlds from nescience and night.

Oh from the rearward of my mind's abyss
Let me bring forth the monstrous thought of bliss!
This is the mother-root of all creation –
Projection, maintenance and consummation.
Spring is the source of each green-thrusting thing,
And Summer's source: this is the source of Spring.
This is the breath, for better or for worse,
In the huge body of the universe,
Impelling it to motions vague and vast,
Of which, as none was first, shall none be last.
Love's rose unfolds its petals but for this,
Winnowing the circumambient air of bliss.
Even the lily white of chastity
Springs from this hidden root to breathe and be
On the bright brink of immortality.
Even the saint, in sunwardness of soul
Soaring and singing as he sights the goal,
Fledged the far winging of his eagle thought
In this rich mother-nest which all forth-brought.
But when the thought sinks in
   As waters from a fountain rise and fall,
Ending where they did begin,
   Or as the rain from clouds purpúreal

Falls on the fields which once as dew it pearled,
Thought's refluent flood falls back from all the beaches of
    the world,
Leaving them dry and bare.
Retreating o'er itself into the deep
Wherefrom its youthful waves did erstwhile leap
Into the broad bright air,
It falls into itself from everywhere.
From every object of the mind
Whose borrowed light has power to blind,
From God's existence and its own
As easily as from a stone,
The outward thought, now taught by pain,
Runs back into the natal brain,
And draws into a point vibrating
With energy for more creating.
But even this is hushed and stilled
If so the almighty mind has willed;
Even this shall disappear
Like a ripple in a mere.
Ah, how calm the lake tonight!
The trees how still! the moon how bright!
And moonlight over all with infinite delight!

THE TAOIST TEACHER

I did not seek, and so I found;
I travelled rooted to the ground.
Words that in jest I uttered here
Were wisdom in the heavenly sphere.

The Secret of the Universe,
Disputed oft in prose and verse,
I never bothered much about –
And that was how I found it out.

All men's questions and replies
Are sometimes foolish, sometimes wise.
I never asked or answered aught –
And that way I both learned and taught.

If you wish to learn of me
Forget all this immediately;
Forget there's such a thing to do –
And then perchance I'll wink at you.

'WATER FROM THE THAWED-OUT SNOW...'

Water from the thawed-out snow
Trickles to streamlets far below;
Joining with rivers strong and free
It pours at last into the sea.

It loitered not among the sedges,
Nor hung in rainbows over ledges;
It kissed the pebbles as it went,
And yet to go it was content.

Oh keep like water in its flow
The pristine purity of snow;
With deeper currents, swifter streams,
Descending through our land of dreams.

Loiter in no stagnant pool,
Though mossy banks are green and cool;
Sport not long with flags and flowers,
Or swallows in the willow-bowers.

The sea our goal, the snow our source –
Such is our appointed course,
Flowing with sunbeam-spangled motion
Calmly to the moonlit ocean.

TO A POLITICAL FRIEND

Thine is the outward action,
Mind is the peace within;
You forge the chains of faction,
I strive to wear them thin.

Through no dissensions narrow
Did you thus dearly go
With the swiftness of an arrow
From the stillness of this bow.

When your hot blood is abating
And anxious thoughts begin
You will feel me meditating,
And peace shall fold us in.

When the limit of your action
And the limit of my peace
Are joined by strong attraction
Our separate selves shall cease.

TO CHENREZI

Lord, from my shadows do I flee
Into Thy lovely light:
To sin's black dross that beauty seems
A furnace fierce and bright;
But its cool light shines on virtue
Like the moon on flowers by night.

Thou smilest, gentle, on those saints
Who tread the Noble Way;
But fierce and furious dost Thou scowl
On fools who walk astray;
These, with a lotus, do You bless,
These, with a sword, You slay.

Teach me to see beyond, Lord,
Thine aspects sweet or stern;
Let my soul not fear destruction,
Nor yet for blessings yearn:
May I leave behind all names and forms
When to Thy light I turn.

LINES

From the unlocked cage of my heart
White doves of love go winging,
Wild larks of song rise singing,
The ice of my heart is broken, broken,
Joy's fountain leaps in the air;
And all the while no word was spoken:
I only looked at something fair.

MEDITATION   *1947*

Here perpetual incense burns;
The heart to meditation turns,
And all delights and passions spurns.

A thousand brilliant hues arise,
More lovely than the evening skies,
And pictures paint before our eyes.

All the spirit's storm and stress
Is stilled into a nothingness,
And healing powers descend and bless.

Refreshed, we rise and turn again
To mingle with this world of pain,
As on roses falls the rain.

THE WHEEL OF DHARMA

Roll forth, O Conquering Wheel,
And cross both land and sea;
Love is more strong than steel,
And hate must yield to thee.
Roll forth on thy victorious course,
And set the nations free from force.

Before thy sun-like sweep
The hosts of Mara fly
Like wan stars to the deep
When Dawn impearls the sky.
Thy splendour spreads from zone to zone —
Roll forth, and make the earth thy own.

Conquer the hearts of men
With love intense, profound;
And penetrate that den
Of darkness underground,
Where, in the midst of shadows deep,
Lust and hate and folly sleep.

Ascend into the sky
And like the sun at noon
Shed radiance from on high —
Thy love's unstinted boon.
When thou hast set the people free
The universe will worship thee.

MUSIC AT NIGHT

The noise of day is hushed at last,
A cool wind softly blows,
And nightingales make beautiful
The silence of the rose.

Stilled is the storm of passion,
And anxious thoughts depart.
Sweet voices do but make more deep
The silence of my heart.

THE WANDERING SINGER

It was the season after rain:
Our feet were cold upon the floor;
A chill wind breathed against the pane;
White mist crept through the door.
With shawls drawn round our shoulders, we
Conned books of deep divinity,
And saints' and sages' subtle lore
Passed our studious eyes before.

We scarce marked, through the cold blue glass,
The flickering stars all frosty white,
Or mountain-muffling cloudlets pass
Across the face of night;
Nor heard, or hearing did not heed,
The faint sound of a far off reed,
Through rising mist and drizzling rain
Sobbing like a soul in pain.

The dust of books was blown away
By breaths of new, yet ancient, song;
A pipe shrilled at the close of day
To voice both sweet and strong.
What though the harlot at our door
Little knows of sages' lore!
Her song, so artless and so wild,
Voices a wisdom undefiled.

Piping and singing fade away,
And melts the mist upon the hills;
Bright in the silver moonlight play
The river's thousand rills.
Now from the mist-admitting door
We watch two shadows flitting o'er
The neighbour ridge and, listening, hear
Both pipe and song again rise clear.

Before some other hut she sings,
Base scion of an ancient art,
Whose voice has power to pluck those strings
That tremble in the heart.
Though sings she at some distant door
My heart shall hearken as before,
And race-deep memories rise to greet
That world-old song so wild and sweet.

THE CLOUDED DRAGON

Behold the Clouded Dragon –
Imperial, gold, benign,
Clad in thunder, eyed with lightning,
Rushing madly, scales ashine,
Down to Earth and up to Heaven
With energy divine –
Soaring, plunging, rolling, twisting
With force all furious-fine.

Behold the Clouded Dragon
As he breasteth, strong and free,
The immensities of Heaven
And the tumult of the sea:
Then draws his clouds around him,
And his cloudlets quietly,
As into mist and pelting rain
He melts mysteriously.

Behold the Clouded Dragon
As a symbol, as a sign,
Of the Sage whose thoughts are thunders,
Whose intuitions shine
Like lightnings in the dark blue sky,
Blinding to mortal eyne;
While he feels the Central Silence
In the storm of the divine.

Behold the Clouded Dragon,
This Sage who smiles at thee;
Follow his furious footsteps,
Win his tranquillity.
His thoughts he draws around him,
For his True Form, fierce and free,
Half hidden by his wisdom,
No man may ever see.

BEFORE AN IMAGE OF THE BUDDHA

What thoughts are present to Thy mind
In that Beyondless State, refined
Through ceaseless discipline and pain
From the crude stuff of flesh and brain;
Or is no thought presént to Thee
At all, in that Infinity?
Looking, in this lonely place,
On Thy silent, sculptured face,
In whose proximity do cease
All unquiet thoughts, and melt in peace,
I struggle, with my little wit,
To fathom out, whilst here I sit,
The calm which beautifieth it
As full moon, on a summer's night,
Silvers still waters with her light.
Thy Sea of Peace is too profound
For plummet of our thought to sound;
Yet, from smooth brow and half-closed eyes,
And silent lips, void of replies,
From coolness and tranquillity
Made palpable to us in Thee,
Our groping minds may somehow guess
That Plenitude yet Emptiness,
That state of passionless Delight,
Mastered by Thee on Wesak Night;
May see, and for a moment sense,
Love, which is Wisdom's effluence,
And feel our being's tiniest part
Beat with the beating of Thy Heart –

Feel too, like Thee, each tear of woe
Fall on our hearts like fire on snow.
O may we, contemplating Thee,
Be lost in that Immensity
Of Peace and Bliss which now Thou art,
And realize the Buddha-Heart!

THE MOON OF BEAUTY

When Truth and Good like phantoms fade
Into the reddening West,
My Moon of Beauty rises soft
To soothe an aching breast.

When Reason's lamp grows dim and faint,
And Aspiration's wing
Beats feebly on the starless dark,
I take my pipe and sing.

For Beauty, whether seen or heard –
When Truth nor Goodness can –
May woo the weary heart from tears
And soothe the grief of man.

NIGHT THOUGHTS*

Across the vastness of the sky
White continents of cloud are spread;
From bank to bank the moon doth ply
Her silver traffic overhead.

Below me, is a single world;
Above, ten thousand million are.
The moon her silver sail has furled
To anchor near the Morning Star.

Each world a million million lives
Contains, yet all with all are one –
The humblest flower of grass that thrives
Is sister to the regnant sun.

Yet must my heart recoil from these
As the burnt hand jerketh from the fire,
And seek within, to find without,
Peace, and cessation of desire.

The moon tonight is bright and new,
Her sail is trimmed to journey far –
The realm of thought I travel to
Is worlds beyond the Morning Star.

Lo, on a starry foaming borne,
Fast paling now, no longer bright,
She strikes the fiery Rock of Dawn
And founders in a sea of light.

That Moon for which I journey far
Shall never wax, wane, or be spent,
And anchors near no Morning Star –
The Full Moon of Enlightenment.

RAIN

How sweet it is, how sweet again
To hear and see and smell the rain!
The birds take shelter in the trees
And sway with the bough that sways with the breeze
As the big drops fall from the silver sky
On the fields of rice that all withered lie.

The peasant shelters, with smiles of relief,
Beneath the broad green plantain leaf.
Sweet to that son of toil to see
The fair rain falling fresh and free;
While on his body, bright with sweat,
The soft cool breeze blows sweeter yet.

The channels fill, then overflow,
As the sweet rain slants to the earth below.
Each blade of grass is bright with gems;
Each grove of palms wears diadems.
The crimson streaks of the western sky
In the glassy fields reflected lie.

Praise to the rain, that falleth fine
On field and tree, on flower and vine:
Praise to the labourers in the sun,
Who rest not till the day is done:
Praise to our patient Mother Earth,
Who gave to us our common birth.

THE PARABLE OF THE PLOUGH

Where green and purple strips of earth
Stretched to far hills of misty blue,
He walked with slow and solemn step
That sanctified the flowers and dew.

The sun shone fiercely white above
And darted down its quivering flame,
As through the new-ploughed fields the Lord
Of Wisdom and Compassion came.

Two milk-white oxen drew the plough
With meek, boughed heads that seemed to hear
The sighful rustle of the palms
And the dry clods breaking in their rear.

The peasant drove the ploughshare deep
Which two strong hands did strictly guide.
Lo, as he turned his docile team,
The silent Lord was at his side.

He knelt with joined, uplifted palms;
His eyes with tears of joy were dim.
And while he knelt, his oxen seemed
To bow their patient heads with him.

The Lord in mercy sweetly spake –
No hour for high discourses now;
He spoke of simple, homely things,
And parabled upon the plough.

By that so gracious accent, all
The humble ways of field and fold –
Ploughing, sowing, reaping, threshing –
Were touched as though with rays of gold.

Yea, as the Lord discoursed to him,
The hardy peasant quickly saw
In lives of clod, flower, beast and man,
The workings of a common law.

Three milk-white blooms the peasant plucked
And with them touched the Blessed Feet.
'I take my refuge, Lord, in Thee,
Thy Doctrine, and Thine Order meet'.

The Lord stepped o'er the thread-thin stream
And went His calm and solemn way.
The ploughman, joyful, gripped his plough,
And plied a whip of song that day.

'ABOVE ME BROODS...'

Above me broods
A world of mysteries and magnitudes.
I see, I hear,
More than what strikes the eye or meets the ear.

Within me sleep
Potencies deep, unfathomably deep,
Which, when awake,
The bonds of life, death, time and space will break.

Infinity
Above me like the blue sky do I see.
Below, in me,
Lies the reflection of infinity.

ASPIRATION 1948

The dim sun sinks to rest
In a west of watery gold.
The young stars climb the sky
And there like flowers unfold,
In the forest vast of night,
Petals of purest light.

So may my heart unfold,
When the suns of the world have set,
In the forest vast of the Void,
Wisdom with Mercy met
In that tranquil, silent hour,
Like a flower and the scent of a flower.

HIMALAYAN SAGES

Those who have hid themselves on heights of snow,
Face to face with the stars and the silver moon,
Shall read upon the rocks the Ancient Rune
And thus decipher secrets. They shall know —
Far from the lips of any earthly lover —
What the mists hide and what the winds discover.

And, with grave eyes of wisdom, they shall scan —
Pitting terrific wills against th' Unknown,
Wringing its secret out of every stone —
The origin and destiny of man;
Shall see a hundred thousand ages roll
Through one brief instant of the human soul.

They shall know utter peace. They shall not feel —
Immersed, upon those constellated peaks,
In that deep joy whereof no language speaks —
The bitterness and bite of brandished steel.
The tumult of the world rolls on and on:
They shall not hear or heed it. They have gone

Afar upon that path which no man knoweth
Save who can frailties and passions tread
Underfoot, leave the living and the dead
For snowy heights whereon no green grass groweth,
And, meditating there, intensify
Th' electric urge to thrust beyond the 'I'.

THE FOUR SIGHTS

Yashodhara
Lord of the black locks, lord of thy handmaid,
Lord of the clouded but beautiful brow,
Lord of all music, lord of all laughter,
Why dost thou ponder so mournfully now?

Say, has some new blossom-shaft of the love god
Wounded the heart that once beat but for me,
Or, dost thou think that the white flame within me
Burneth for one more beloved than thee?

Here in these gardens where fountains are falling,
With the green grass beneath, and the blue sky above,
Where we hover like bees round the blossom of beauty,
No sorrows may come but the sorrows of love.

Lift up thy sad eyes, and see in the heavens
The moon in her beauty, the stars with their light.
Now, while the soft wind blows heavy with perfume,
Dost thou not think of the pleasures of night?

Oh why dost thou stir not, why dost thou speak not,
Why do thy mute lips vouchsafe no reply?
Though heavy as death be the sorrow that bows thee,
Yea, thy beloved must share it or die.

Siddhartha
Pity may move me, though passion may never,
To open the source of my sorrow to thee,
Folding back petal on petal of pining,
As the flower shows its heart at the hest of the bee.

Our love which, as jasmine, grew fragrant at nightfall,
When sweet-voiced musicians were tuning the string,
Had a cool palace roof for the heat of the Summer,
A palace for Winter, a palace for Spring.

With wreaths of blue lotus our black locks adorning,
With garments of muslin and garlands of rose,
Day after day in the gay painted chamber,
In the season of flowers, in the season of snows;

Month after month in the green parks of pleasaunce,
At morning the orchards, at evening the bowers,
No joy was unknown there, no pleasure untasted,
When lamplight and starlight and moonlight were
    ours.

But now, the delights of the couch and the garden,
The collar of turquoise, the chaplet of pearls,
The hymns of the poet, the hope of a kingdom,
The stripling musicians, the chorus of girls,

Even thy moon-apple breasts, my beloved,
Thy swan-like demeanour, thy sweetness in talk,
Thy kohl and thy carmine, delight me no longer,
Like blossoms which wither when cropped from the stalk.

For of late as I raced through the streets of the city,
With flying white horses all hurrying-hoar,
Three sights did I see – things common as kisses –
But it seemed I had never beheld them before.

The first sight I saw was a grey-bearded grandsire,
Withered and weak who was blooming and strong,
His slow, painful steps on a bamboo supporting,
Creeping and wheezing and mumbling along.

The second a man who lay wasted with fever,
Burning yet freezing, fighting for breath,
Twitching and trembling, his features distorted,
As fearful and frantic he wrestled with death.

The third sight I saw as I whirled through the city,
With stiff, lifeless hands, its blank face upturned,
Borne on a bedstead, by mourners surrounded,
Was a grim, silent corpse on its way to be burned.

Then, as the silver-white beauty of morning
Springs from the mountains and dapples the skies,
Chasing the goblins and ghosts with its arrows,
A fourth sight, beloved, confronted my eyes.

Lord of his senses, lord of his thinking,
Humble yet mighty, lowly but high,
A monk in pure beauty outshining the many
As the full moon the host of the stars in the sky.

These three sights of sorrow have soberly shown me,
Pitiless-plain as the midsummer sky,
That in spite of their youth and their beauty of body
All men must wither and sicken and die.

This is the source of the sorrow that bows me,
Making me weary of music and flowers,
Making my heart in its anguish not heeding
The call of the orchards, the bliss of the bowers.

The fourth sight I saw by the roadside has taught me,
Simple-sublime as the mountains of snow,
That forth from my house to the fear-haunted forest
To solve these dark riddles of life I must go.

And I know not of months, weeks or days now the number
The flag of a prince shall for me be unfurled,
Ere I go forth to seek for a way to the Deathless
With heart of compassion, the hope of the world.

SONNET

Aloft the many-petalled lotus rears
From sunlit water its pure beauty white;
And shining presences adore the sight
Of Him Who sits upon it, free from fears;
For, having tasted the sharp salt of tears,
Back to the bitter springs of false delight
He tracked through transformations infinite
The lust that lures men into births and biers.

Oh to the multitude of gods and men
Do Thou reveal in every faultless part
The Law that leads to Peace most radiant –
Love beyond love, Light beyond light – and then
Sit Thou upon the lotus of my heart,
O Lord, and teach me, being ignorant.

WESAK JOY

The swiftest, sweetest pen could ne'er indite
What joy Thou hadst upon that Wesak Night;
And though a voice such as the stars may have
Should breast all music as a swan the wave
And bear on to the utmost verge of sound,
They could not utter forth Thy joy profound.
And this I know; for now, by following Thee
With first weak steps to Perfect Purity,
I bear within my heart a mite of bliss,
And bearing, cannot even utter this.

THE SUN-PATH

Adiccapathehamsa yanti
DHAMMAPADA

Swanlike, upon the Sun-Path let me soar
To That which lives beyond the Threefold Veil,
Leaving this weed-choked pond for evermore
Fringed with sweet-fuming poisonous poppies pale.

I follow One Love-Winged and Wisdom-Eyed
Who first upon that Path did soar and see
The rending of the Threefold Veil, and cried
Before He passed Beyond, 'Oh follow me!'

The clear, sweet music of His Victory-Song
Rainlike from far away and long ago
Falls on their hearing and their hearts who long
Swanwise upon that Solar Path to go.

Pierced by the arrows of a millions stars,
Through banks of cloud, through darkness absolute,
Through gulfs of soundlessness no music mars,
Past suns the reeling brain might ne'er compute;

Onward and upward with aspiring wing
Undaunted through a myriad worlds they press –
Now in the Realm of Beauty bosoming,
Now floating in the Vast of Nothingness.

Oh last and least of all that glorious train,
Though feeble-winged and fearful, may I be!
Let me not paddle in the Pool of Pain,
Nor ruffle to the Wind of Transiency!

Leaving the mud-flats of mortality,
With flight unwearied, faith that may not fail,
Not swerving from the Sun-Path, may I see
At last the rending of the Threefold Veil.

With crowding suns and moons left far behind,
That Bliss and Peace which now they cannot guess,
My wings, for ever folded, there shall find,
Upon the sapphire Lake of Deathlessness.

ADVENT

I listened all day for the knock of the Stranger,
And I often looked out from the door.
The table was scrubbed, the brass shining,
And well swept the floor.

The shadows grew longer and longer,
In the grate the fire flickered and died.
'It's too late. He never will come now'
I said, and sighed.

I sat there musing and musing,
The spinning-wheel still at my side.
The moonlight came in through the window
White like a bride.

As the clock struck twelve I heard nothing
But *felt* He had come and stayed
Waiting outside. And I listened –
And I was afraid.

SECRET WINGS

We cry that we are weak although
We will not stir our secret wings;
The world is dark — because we are
Blind to the starriness of things.

We pluck our rainbow-tinted plumes
And with their heaven-born beauty try
To fledge nocturnal shafts, and then
Complain 'Alas! we cannot fly!'

We mutter 'All is dust' or else
With mocking words accost the wise:
'Show us the Sun which shines beyond
The Veil' — and then we close our eyes.

To powers above and powers beneath
In quest of Truth men sue for aid,
Who stand athwart the Light and fear
The shadow that themselves have made.

Oh cry no more that you are weak
But stir and spread your secret wings,
And say 'The world is bright, because
We glimpse the starriness of things.'

Soar with your rainbow plumes and reach
That near-far land where all are one,
Where Beauty's face is aye unveiled
And every star shall be a sun.

THE TRAMP

I will not read the scriptures
Of advertisements obscene;
I will not offer incense
To the godhead of Machine;
I will not be a pawn in
The game of politics;
I will *not* sell my birthright;
I *will* kick against the pricks.

Not in tired but sleepless cities
Where the black smoke shrouds the stars;
Not in the reeking rottenness
Of brothels and of bars;
Not in office or in workshop
Where, labouring night and day,
The sullen millions languish,
One second will I stay.

I will read the Book of Nature
That reveals the things above;
I will offer my heart's incense
To Wisdom and to Love;
I will fill my life with beauty
And with joy transfigure it;
I will rise and claim my birthright
And to Truth alone submit.

By willow-shaded waters
From village snug not far;
On slow-trailed creaking barges
Beneath the Evening Star;
In fields, by hill or valley,
Contented, night and day,
With birds and flowers and butterflies
For ever will I stay.

SRI PADA 1949

I saw His shining footprints
Gleaming in the grass like dew;
The flowers, where they had fallen,
Sweeter and fairer grew:
They led into the distant hills,
Those hills all misty-blue.

I will follow, I will follow,
'Neath the Spring Moon full and bright,
Through field and copse and hollow,
Those footprints of delight,
And walk upon those distant hills
One dawn all golden-white.

'Tis many an age of darkness
Since the days my Lord did pass
Leaving His dewy footprints
Like pearls upon the grass,
And rank weeds have o'ergrown them,
And thorns obscured, alas!

Yet will I follow boldly,
Using the hunter's art,
Until one day I find Him,
From all things else apart,
Sitting beside the Pool of Peace
In the blue hills of my heart.

THE POET'S REPLY

'With your holy vows,
Your shaven head,
And your stitched-stuff robes
Ensaffronéd,
How can you sing still?'
The people said.

They pointed fingers
Of scorn at me.
'A true ascetic
He cannot be;
For his lips are stained
With poesy.'

'Poor fools', I replied,
'These songs of mine
Are the rapturous lilt
Of the life divine;
But yours are tainted
With lust and wine.

'If a song-bird caged
Can sing merrily,
With its wings close clipped
(And such are ye),
Oh how much sweeter
'Twill sing when free!'

'TIRED OF THE CRIMSON CURTAIN...'*

Tired of the crimson curtain,
Tired of the gilded chair,
Tired of the scented bosom,
Tired of the loosened hair,
I went into the garden
To breathe the sunlit air.

I heard the drowsy murmur
Of flower-emerging bees;
Before the holy Passion Flower
I sank on both my knees;
I talked on Art with tulips;
I fell in love with trees.

Crazed by incessant searches
In the Wilderness of Word,
Crazed by close-printed volumes
Whose dust lies aye unstirred,
I stole into a thicket
To hear a singing-bird.

Perched on a spray of roses
She poured into my ear
The sorrow of the nightingales
For Ítylus so dear,
The ecstasies of skylarks,
The lusts of chanticleer.

Maddened with thirst for being,
Maddened with circling round
In the vortex of existence,
Baffled, blinded, bound,
I cast aside three bodies
Which in three worlds are found.

Like an avalanche descended
Unbounded ecstasy;
Unending vistas opened out
Into eternity;
The Ocean of Nirvana
Swallowed the droplet 'me'.

PEACE

Turn away from the world, weary pilgrim,
There is no rest for thee there;
The quietness of star-communing hills
'Twere better for thee to share;
In the silence that lies at the forest's heart
Breathes a peace beyond compare.

In glades where Spring-buds quicken
When frosts no more appal,
In fields and leafy by-lanes red
With ripened fruits of Fall,
The leaves, now green, now yellow, teach
That change must come to all.

Comes peace more cool than the moonlight is
That silvers the gliding stream,
When the stilled heart knows, in the forest depths,
The world is an empty dream,
And turns with delight to the Things That Are
From the things that merely seem.

THE WORD OF THE BUDDHA

If thirst for truth doth like a fire
Consume thy soul in every part,
Oh quench it with the words that pour
In streams from His Himálayan heart.

From heights of Vision crowned with stars,
Cleaving the thunderous clouds of strife,
Those waters pour to fructify
The barren fields of human life.

Oh questing hearts who have not known
How rich those precious waters are,
In every azure wavelet gleams
A pearl more brightly than a star.

Forsake the fen of sickly thoughts,
Which now thy heart doth so entrance,
Where croak the frogs of doubt, where bloom
The purple flowers of ignorance,

And journeying to those green-turfed banks
Stand breathless on the moonlit beach,
And see and hear beneath the stars
The mighty river of His Speech.

Oh sun-scorched pilgrim, drink at last
Those waters pure from snow to sea –
Those jewelled waves which are to men
The Draught of Immortality.

WESAK THOUGHTS

Since that auspicious Full-Moon Day
Which saw Thy pangless birth,
How many bloodstained centuries
Have stormed across the earth.

Across her green and pleasant face,
More savage than the lion
How many conquerors have rolled
Their chariots of iron.

How many battles lost and won,
How many cities razed;
How many a trail with fire and sword
Through town and village blazed.

But here and there, like halcyon birds
That nest upon the flood,
Or like to azure lotuses
Blooming in pools of blood,

The Winners of the Paths and Fruits
In many an age and clime –
Throughout the islands of the East –
Have taught Thy Truth sublime.

On Ganges' silver-sanded shores
Full many a Sage hath seen
The Truths of Ill, its Cause, its Cure,
And trod the Path between.

In forest bower and mountain cave,
Remote from passions vile,
How many Saints illustrious made
The copper-coloured Isle.

The Country of the Yellow Robe
Was rich in days of old
With many a Seer more precious than
Her rubies and her gold.

On dizzying peaks, in blinding snows,
How many Dauntless Ones
Have seen the dawning of a Light
More glorious than the sun's.

In China's dragon-haunted land
The heirs of Truth and Art
Have pictured with a brush inspired
The moonlight of the heart.

And Isles that greet the rising sun
Have glimpsed upon the wing
Enlightenment more beautiful
Than cherry trees in Spring.

In these and many other lands,
Where hearts were erst on fire
With lust, Thy sons, O Lord, have known
The bliss on non-desire.

When hatred like a tidal wave
Engulfed the coral isles
Of peace, Thy sons with love have swept
It back a hundred miles.

Oh here and now how great the need
For Sage and Saint and Seer!
Oh when will Metteyya come, Oh when
Will Arahants appear?

For now upon the roofless world
The floods of sorrow pour;
Like dreadful, distant thunderclouds
Are heard the drums of war.

With leprous fingers interclasped
And blood-stiff garments sere,
From heart to heart with crimson steps
Stalk lust and hate and fear.

Tormented on his bed of pain
With many a grievous ill,
Mankind must now or never use
The Great Physician's skill.

Now with its clear, triumphant voice
Must sound, as ne'er before,
In all the quarters of the earth,
The Trumpet of the Law.

Though in this world that now must pluck
The bitterest fruits of sin,
The reign of hate will cease one day,
The reign of love begin,

Not from blue cloud or silver star
Will love be wafted then,
But from the self-same place where hate
Was born — the hearts of men.

Oh now must Ganges' silver shores,
The copper-coloured Isle,
The Country of the Yellow Robe,
Each peak and snowy pile,

With China's dragon-haunted land
And Isles that greet the sun
At morn, and other islands, see
Once more Nirvana won.

In North and South, in East and West,
In house or hermitage,
The Lord's disciples ceaseless war
With Mara's hosts must wage.

With ardent hearts and tireless hands,
On Truth's foundation sure,
Vow, friends, to build upon the earth
The City of the Law.

Nerve your strong hearts and steel your wills
For conquest over pain;
Desire uproot unflinchingly
The Deathless to attain.

And then across the verdant earth,
Which erst iron chariots saw,
Will sunlike roll from East to West
The glorious Wheel of Law.

And rising in its azure track
Will beam with rich increase
The moon that men are pining for –
The Wesak Moon of peace.

TO THE RECUMBENT BUDDHA

Mahaparinibbana Temple, Kusinara

Thou art not dead, nor dost Thou even sleep
Here on this solemn couch of flower-strewn gold;
But lying plunged in meditation deep
Dost with a peace ineffable enfold
All who with pilgrim footsteps wend to Thee
Sick of the world, and longing to be free.

Couched on my knees before Thy figure vast,
Soothed by the stillness of this silent place,
After much striving I behold at last
The lamp-illumined beauty of Thy face,
And, trembling, feel around, below, above,
The pulsing of Thy vibrant peace and love.

Though witless ones may deem asleep or dead
One who hath shuffled off this mortal form,
O Winner of the Deathless, Thou hast said
Thou livest on for ever in Thy Norm,
And therethrough with unconquerable might
Dost guide the worlds along the path of light.

For in this low-ceiled chamber throbs a heart
Which never was, nor ever will be, still;
But must, like dew, invisibly impart
Its fruit-maturing influence, until
Men feel its pulse in every quickened vein
Strong as the Spring-tides of the moon-charmed main.

Still through this tomb-quiet temple thrills that voice,
In accents by the sensual ear unheard,
Which once the triple world did so rejoice
With its immaculate, majestic word
That taught the origin and end of pain,
And which to this sick world must teach again.

Not in this solitary cell alone,
Not in soft whispers to the faithful heart,
Not with stiff, gilded hand and lips of stone,
But loud in busy street and bustling mart
Through living, breathing lips Thy truth must be
Proclaimed with love by those who follow Thee.

Flicker the lamps. The incense, ashen-white,
Distils no more its tribute of perfume.
On Thine unblinking eyes and visage bright
I gaze with love before I quit the room.
Thy still lips whisper, soft as wind in grass,
'My son, despair not: it shall come to pass.'

THE WOUNDED SWAN

Out of the sunset with the Evening Star,
And with eve's long blue shadows falling down
Into the lotus bed which hides our bower,
Behold, my love, I come again to thee.

O wild thy shriek, O terrible thy grief,
When from the royal swan-flight reeling down,
A mass of fluttering feathers, wing-transpierced,
I fell with bloody plumage to the ground.

How gentle was the hand that smoothed my neck,
How pitiful the eyes that gazed on me,
How musical the voice that sadly said
'Alas, poor bird, what have they done to thee!'

He bore me on his breast with boundless love,
And though the evil prince who brought me down
Came proudly with his friends to claim his prize
The arms that clasped me would not let me go.

With heart pressed close to beating heart we went
Into the perfumed chambers of the king –
I with the prince's muslin round my wing,
He with the wild swan's blood upon his clothes.

And there the king in council did decree
That the poor wounded life of right belonged
Not to the cruel hand that brought it low
But to the loving one that raised it up.

Laid on a bed of azure lotuses,
Fed on delicious honey, fruits and milk,
And tended by the hands that rescued me,
My pulse of life began to throb again.

And often, as he stooped to smooth my wing,
The prince would murmur like a wind in reeds,
Pressing his tear-bright cheek against my neck,
'Alas, the grief that comes to living things!'

And often, when the moon was full and bright,
Wrapped in the purple shadows of a tree
Whose boughs spread out against the stars, the prince
Would sit and muse upon the woes of men.

Though rich the fragrant chambers where he dwelt
With softly burning lamps and blazing jewels,
I think the prince was far less happy there
Than we two are in this blue lotus bower.

For when, what time my stricken wing was healed
And all its silver plumage bright again,
I took once more the freedom of the skies,
The sad prince almost seemed to envy me.

Into the sunrise with the Morning Star
And with the mists of evening rising up
Above the pale gold clouds, I sought once more
This silver tarn set in these dark blue hills.

Bright as the heaven with stars doth seem this bed
Of azure lotuses agleam with dew,
And like a bank of moonlit clouds our nest,
And therein like the moon of Autumn thou.

Far higher than the starry arch of heaven,
And deeper than the distant emerald seas,
Far brighter than the brightest Autumn moon,
Far stronger than our love, his love for me.

Before the sunrise blushes through the East,
Before the fields are bright with morning dew,
Before the sad prince, rising from his couch,
Beholds the swan-deserted lotus bed,

O come, my love, and wing to wing with me
Flash like a silver arrow through the night,
Down from the blue hills like a shooting star
Into the prince's azure lotus pool.

There let us build again our reedy bower
And glitter in the moonlight of his love –
Love higher than the starry arch of heaven
And deeper than the distant emerald seas.

THE FACE OF SILENCE

Before me through the evening air
With robes of saffron hue
And one lean, sunbrowned shoulder bare
And shadow long and blue

He went. I watched him till he turned
A turning of the road.
The West one golden glory burned
And all the treetops glowed.

With such a flood of beauty came
The setting sun that day
That him who walked as though in flame
Before me on the way

I quite forgot. The stars of night
Like silver doves did seem
On the bare branches to alight –
I thought that I did dream.

Then at that turning as I turned
Where he had turned before
When all the trees like torches burned,
At the tree-root I saw

Him sitting on a grassy space
Poised in some lofty swoon:
On his still form and peaceful face
Shone bright the broad full moon.

All breathlessly and silently
With awe I tiptoed near;
And yet — he looked so peacefully —
I had no sense of fear.

O'er his still features breathed a calm
I had not seen before.
It drew me as some maiden's charm
A lover to her door.

The light he saw I could not see,
And yet it seemed to glow
Upon his face more beauteously
Than sunlight on the snow.

At last I turned away, and blessed
The womb that gave him birth,
Knowing that there in truth was rest
And peace for those on earth.

THE LORD OF COMPASSION

In the midnight of the dense ignorance of the world the flower of Thy Compassion blossomed like a great golden lotus on the unruffled surface of the waters of Thy Mind,
Whilst the Full Moon of Thine Enlightenment hung overhead in the azure heavens ablaze with stars…
The wind that bore freezingly from the bare hills and leafless forests shrill voices of grief, shrieks of pain, sobs of despair,
Returning, blew back thither warm with the infinite fragrance of the unfolding petals of the great golden lotus of Thy Love…
Though that Full Moon is no more seen gloriously bright in the azure heavens amidst a host of blazing stars, and though that wondrous blossom long since closed its dawny petals bright,
Still through the moonless, starless darkness of the midnight of the dense ignorance of the world
Is wafted, O Lord of Compassion, the exceeding sweetness of the fragrance of Thy Love.

TRUTH, LOVE, LIFE AND MAN

Truth is not truth, unless to men it is
A path that guides their winged or weary feet
Up to its heaven-high sublimities
Adazzle with the snowfall, sheet on sheet.
Unless Truth leads men from the dark, it is
Not Truth but only words, and false as sweet.

Love is not Love, unless to all it is
Free as the air, impartial as the sun,
And leaveth not, to dote on deities
Unreal, the creatures real it could have won.
Unless Love feels for all alike, it is
Not Love for any, but desire for one.

Life is not Life, unless to joy it is
A bringer of swift death, to grief a friend,
Or if it spoils not bliss with agonies,
Teaching that sweetest things have soonest end.
Unless Life teach, and we learn this, it is
Not Life but mere existence that we've kenned.

Man is not Man, unless to Truth he is
A pilgrim pledged who tries with might and main
To scale its dazzling-white divinities,
With boundless love for those who tread the plain.
Unless Man strives for Truth and loves, he is
Not Man but merely brute, and lives in vain.

THE MESSAGE OF THE BOWL

Hardly in words these lips can tell
Those noons I recollect so well,
When, after many a dusty mile
Which talk did something to beguile,
We entered, glad of coolth and breeze,
A dense green grove of mango trees,
Unslung our bowls, then bright as glass,
And after resting on soft grass
Tow'rd neighbouring village took our way –
A village all of thatch and clay;
And there, past many a straggling row
Of mud-walled cabins cramped and low,
Past tiled and timbered mansions which
Carved post and portico made rich,
Bearing our alms-bowls, quietly went
Questing the heart's enlightenment.
Yea, with the hope of winning truth,
And to curb the flame-fierce pride of youth,
We moved in silence from door to door
And begged from the poorest of the poor.
The white kine eyed us as we passed,
And wide-eyed children stared aghast,
While women pitied, as women must,
The strangers covered with heat and dust;
And old men, roused from noontide beds,
Watched and wondered and shook their heads.
Cool courtyards smeared with cowdung clean
We entered noiseless and unseen,
And there in silence stood before
The little, low, unlintelled door,

Till someone stirred within, and came
To ask our need, and grant the same.
Oh, to the poor the poor are kind,
Sharing their board with lowly mind.
If in receiving I could be
Humble as they in giving me,
Winged would I tread that path of peace
Which uphill winds to the heart's release,
And in this loathsome body find
Immaculate the Buddha-mind.
Those palaces of blue-veined stone
Where pining greatness reigned alone
Behind the jewelled ivory screen,
Where perfumed lamps of amber sheen
As though with moonlight did illume
The barren richness of the room,
Are far less precious in my sight
Than those poor huts, neglected quite,
Of paddy-thatch and sunburnt clay
Where first we begged our food that day;
Nor was my father's house more dear
Than those dark doors wherefrom did peer
The quiet-eyed women, gravely kind,
Who brought the best their hearts could find,
And gave with sweeter, gentler grace
Than ever beamed from beauty's face.
Thin, flat, round cakes of barley-bread
White from the hearth, raw onions red,
Brown country rice, hot chillies, greens,
Chutneys and achars, potherbs, beans,
All, as from door to door we passed,
Into our round-mouthed bowls they cast;

And all, together kneaded, we
Ate 'neath the dense-leaved mango tree.
Ah, and more bliss that almsfood brings
Than all the sugared cates of kings –
Epícurean banquetings!
Then did my deepest heart-thoughts feel
Knit with the poor through woe and weal,
And passionately longed to thrust
Plumed pride into that sacred dust,
And mingling there, foot-trampled, be
Levelled with holiest poverty
Which doth with love enrich the soul,
And spells the Message of the Bowl.

THE CITADEL

Build thou upon thy spirit's mountainous height
Strongholds of Light!
Build with the square white stones of virtuous deed
Mortared with love's rich meed;
Build terraces of loftiest meditations
For watchmen's stations;
And pinnacles of wisdom higher still
Uprear with dauntless skill;
And then command Truth's banner be unfurled
Above the world.

For streaming from their Light-beleaguered coasts
Come Mara's hosts:
Hating that flaming Hand they seek to smite
Direct the Heart of Light;
And tow'rd thy mount from regions far asunder
Their chariots thunder.
Yet fear thou not! the ponderous sword of Good
Was ever unwithstood.
If thou dost guard thine own heart's citadel
All will be well.

THE WHITE CALF

Outstretched upon the sandy ground
Beneath the trees, beneath the stars,
We watched the silver full moon round
Dapple the earth with silver bars.

After long toil and tardy ease
How sweet it was at last to lie
Silent beneath the moon-blanched trees
Feeling the stillness of the sky.

With sleep at last our lids were sealed
And all the night long we had lain,
But loud from heaven the thunder pealed
And down in torrents rushed the rain.

We scrambled up. The stars were fled,
The wind was straining at the trees
And whipping up our sandy bed
In wavelets like a stormy sea's.

Into a narrow shed of clay
With cowdunged and uneven floor
For shelter then we groped our way,
And shivering bedded in the straw.

Chill through the open doorway blew
The wind, and with the wind the rain,
While we, for more we could not do,
Huddled beside the sacks of grain.

Above, the thunder boomed and crashed,
And all without was dark and drear,
Save when the fitful lightning flashed
And showed the tumult we could hear.

At length, by weariness oppressed,
In spite of cold and wind and rain,
Sprawled on the floor with placid breast
We slumbered till 'twas day again.

Then, as the dawn's first rays did fall
Bright through the open doorway wide,
Turning my head, I saw a small
White calf still sleeping at my side.

Nestling upon the same soft straw
As I, with head to hoof, he lay,
So peacefully that one who saw
Could hardly keep the tears away.

To me that small life did impart
A kind of aching tenderness,
Such as may fill a mother's heart
To see her infant's helplessness.

And in the deepest depths of me
I felt that I had understood
In one clear flash the mystery
Of universal brotherhood.

TENDAI

How can I scorn the beggar's lot
When heart and mind have understood
The wayside dust in which he sits
Shall rise to Perfect Buddhahood?

Rather in reverence shall I fold
My hands, the beggar's lot to see.
Hail, Jewel of Enlightenment
Stitched in the hem of poverty!

THE LOTUS OF COMPASSION

The Lotus blooms tonight,
The great golden Lotus of the Lord's Compassion.
With white roots deep in the slime of this sad world,
And huge green leaves spread on the surface of the waters of the
    Lake of Tears,
And surrounded by myriads of silver lotus-buds,
Like white hands folded in prayer for succour from the miseries of
    the world,
That Lotus blooms tonight.
O leave the crowded shore where men buy and sell,
Shake off the soft detaining fingers of your friends,
And in a little boat,
At midnight, when the moon is full,
And glitters at you from the water,
Row swiftly to the quiet Heart of the Lake where the Lotus blooms,
The great golden Lotus of the Lord's Compassion;
And you will feel the sweetness ineffable of its heart-fragrance
Coming on a breeze which ripples the face of the silent waters
To meet you beneath the stars.

THE ONLY WAY
1950

One need, and one need only,
All earthly things above,
This world hath now as ever —
The need of boundless love.

One way, and one way only,
There is to outward peace —
That Great Heart of Compassion
Which bids all sorrows cease.

THE BIRTHPLACE OF COMPASSION

Buddha Gaya, 1949

Here, where the Goatherd's banyan-tree
O'ershadowed, was, to world forlorn,
The first child of Enlightenment,
Compassion, born.

Seeing men bloom like lotus flowers
With petals closed, or half apart,
Her pulses fluttered underneath
The Buddha-Heart.

And when that high and holy hour
With stars shone down upon her birth,
There opened wide a way to peace
For all on earth.

THE FRAGRANCE OF COMPASSION

Seeing this world, this hapless world,
With all its store of woes,
Compassion in the Buddha-Heart
Burst open like a rose.

And from that flower, that wondrous flower,
There came at once to birth
A breath whose perfume even now
With fragrance fills the earth.

ON THE BRINK

Here on the river-brink I sit
Where thick the tall white lily grows,
And feel the clear, cold ripples break
With icy kisses on my toes.

The willows trail their almond leaves
With one side white, and one side green,
Atop the glasswaves tremblingly,
While the shrill wind blows cold and keen.

The waves that nibble at my feet
Are touched with dull, hard glints of gold,
And the shadows of the tired sun
Stretch out more long and black and cold.

The moon, by one white star attended,
Lies on her bright back crescent-thin.
I weep beside the blackening waves
Because I failed to venture in.

INVOCATION

Field-freshening rain,
White night-rain lingering on in drizzles till the dawn,
Pools of bright silver making, birthing streams
In dry clay river-beds, pour down, O rain,
All day, all night, pour down pour down, O rain,
Pour down…

World-welfaring Compassion,
Void-born Compassion diamond-hard and petal-tender,
Peace to wild heartwaves bringing, birthing love
On the low couch of self, pour down, Compassion,
All day, all night, pour down pour down, Compassion,
Pour down –
Pour down like rain on this compassionless
Lost world…

Pour down, pour down, pour down…

THE ALMS OF COMPASSION

In the saffron robe of yearning,
And my heart in my hand for a bowl,
I went from door to door, seeking
Alms for my soul.

Some gave me wealth and pleasure,
Some gave me knowledge and skill,
But the small round heart-bowl in my hand
They could not fill.

And as the hot sun ascended
I went with such weary feet
From door to door and from house to house
Down life's long street.

Nor had I ever found there
The alms that was life to me,
And had died, perhaps, on their doorsteps,
But suddenly

I was ware of a Jewel-Tower standing
Like a flower beside the sea,
And One with face most beautiful
Gave alms to me.

Oh when, at the end of my journey,
I stood in the dusty road
And received the great alms of Compassion
My bowl o'erflowed.

THE UNSEEN FLOWER

Compassion is far more than emotion. It is something that springs
Up in the emptiness which is when you yourself are not there,
So that you do not know anything about it.
Nobody, in fact, knows anything about it
(If they knew it, it would not be Compassion);
But they can only smell
The scent of the unseen flower
That blooms in the Heart of the Void.

VILLAGE INDIA

I have found you, India,
Here in the villages,
In the houses with clay walls and thatched roofs
And ricefields and wheatfields
Green at their doors...
Not in the cities
With their tramways and talkies
From the West mass-imported;
Not in the museums
Behind the long, shining
Rows of glass cases
With brickbats and potsherds;
Not in the temples
Where the smells of decayed flowers
And stale incense mingle,
And garish lights shine on the faces of stone gods,
And coconuts broken, and priests fee-demanding;
Not on the snow-peaks
With hermits in hiding,
Nor yet by the stream-side
In the gardens of poets with flowers –
But here in the villages
Which birthed the great cities,
And filled the museums
With wrought gold and jewelled work
And lingams of silver;
Which flung up the stone walls
Of temples, and scooped out
Their sanctuaries, and lit there
Innumerable rows of lamps before deities,

Splitting coconuts and scattering rice
To fatten the priests;
Which nurtured the hermit
And showed to the eyes of the poet his first sight of beauty –
Here in the villages
Which ploughed, sowed, reaped and threshed
The ricefields and wheatfields
I have found you, India,
At last, and embrace you
And feel on my shoulder
Your cool flowing tresses.

RHYMED TANKA

Mountains bathed in mist
How mysteriously you stand!
But when darkness falls
Deeper on hill after hill
You grow more mysterious still.

RHYMED HAIKU

   On the blue hill-side
Village fires like orange jewels
    Gleam at eventide.

THE LAMP OF COMPASSION

My heart-wick now is charred with sin,
And dully red it glows
With greed or hate, afloat upon
The viscous oil of woes.

Oh may I set it flaming with
Compassion's golden fire,
Which feeds upon the twisted strands
Of anger and desire,

And hold its rainbowed radiance up
In wisdom's crystal vase
To light their way who from this world
Are stumbling to the stars!

MOUNTAINS

Golden in laughing sunlight,
Silver in mist and rain,
I see thee, mighty mountains,
Tower heavenward from the plain,

And pray my heart unmoved by
Sweet joys or sufferings dire,
Like thee through cloud and sunlight
May upward still aspire.

MESSENGERS FROM TIBET*

Whence come these asses, brazen-belled,
That jingle down the dusty lane
With big brown bales of tufty wool –
A hundred in a single train?

Whence comes their master, crimson-cloaked,
Who drives them onward from the rear,
With braided and beribboned locks,
And gold- and turquoise-studded ear?

Whence comes this music, weird and wild,
Of clashing cymbals, tinkling bells,
And trumpets deep that thunder out
The sorrows of a hundred hells?

Whence come these banners, bright as gems,
Above the images unfurled
On shadowy temple walls, that seem
Like glimpses of another world?

Whence come these memories, vague as dreams,
Of peaks where snow eternal reigns,
Of boundless grassy wastes beyond –
The silent Central Asian plains?

Whence comes this yearning, sharp as life,
Strong as death's self, to mount and go
Beyond the hundred-headed hills
High up the sky-ascending snow?

Oh land of turquoise, land of gold,
Land of the whispered, mystic lore,
Land of the Buddha, land unknown,
Were you *my* land in days of yore?

Though dense the mists of birth and death
Your messengers are riding through.
How shall peace fill my heart again
Unless I journey back to you?

BAMBOOS

Among all branched things, I for beauty choose
The yellowness and slimness of bamboos,
Whose bunched leaves twinkle on a gusty day
And back and forth the clattering branches sway.

And when from frozen skies the pure snows fall
In large white flakes that softly mantle all
The loaded branches stoop without a sound
Till their green leaf-tips almost touch the ground.

Then, when they seem a kind of crystal tree
Sparkling with diamond buds and silvery
Shoots, by the snowflakes' overburdening
And their own patience freed, the lithe boughs spring

Up, and in powdery showers the white snow flies
Flung by the wind across the freezing skies,
While, as the bamboos dance in wind and rain,
Like stars the bunched leaves twinkle forth again.

Hence, among branched things I for beauty choose
The yellowness and slimness of bamboos,
Which taught me, more than what in books is writ,
That life is conquered when we yield to it.

STANZAS

Let my life burn like incense
Before Thy precious shrine,
Consuming, for Thy Doctrine's sake,
All thought of 'I' and 'mine';

That from its smouldering selfhood
May rise up unalloyed
The white cloud of compassion –
Pure perfume of the Void.

THE GARDENER

The gardener crops his rose-tree's hundred buds,
That when it grows
Rich with the breath of Summer, it may bear
One perfect rose.

And even so I prune my budding thoughts,
That in me should
Spring sweetly forth the single perfect bloom
Of Buddhahood.

KANCHENJUNGA

One white wave of snow
Towering against the blue
Sky, with clouds below.

RHYMED HAIKU

Below in the deep
Blue valleys the white clouds
Are lying asleep.

THE BODHISATTVA

Because I could not muse apart
In world-oblivious ecstasy,
But felt like fire-drops on my heart
The tears of all humanity,
I cast aside that source of pride
The glittering robe of selfish peace,
And donned the dress of painfulness
Until all others' pain should cease.

In house and market, shop and cell,
Wherever men in bondage be,
Yes, in the very depth of Hell,
My puissant pity sets them free.
Nor shall I cease to strive for peace
Till every trembling blade of grass
That feels with pain the sting of rain
Into Nirvana's bliss shall pass.

Let me endure unending pains,
Drain to the dregs grief's bitterest cup;
While one unhappy life remains
My own I cannot render up.
Nirvana's joy would only cloy
Should it to me alone befall:
Closed evermore Nirvana's door
Unless I enter last of all!

'WHITE MIST DRIFTS DOWN THE VALLEY DIM...'

White mist drifts down the valley dim,
Then spreads and rises noiselessly,
And the blue hill-tops seem to swim
Like islands in a spectral sea.

Swiftly the silver edges rise
Until the white waves overflow
The shadowy hills, and with the skies
Make one vast sheet as though of snow.

One moment all the world seems white,
A pearly whiteness tinged with blue,
Till the fierce storm-gods rush and smite
That sea of massing clouds in two.

Oh when, with darkness overhead,
In two vast waves they roll apart,
A river like a silver thread
Gleams on the valley's azure heart.

LIFE'S FURNACE

As bellows roar, and red coals glow,
And softened silver slowly bends,
Deft chisels, glancing to and fro,
Are fashioning use to beauty's ends.

Life's furnace flames, shower sparks of ill,
In pain the heart doth burn and glow,
As the keen chisel of the will
Shapes final good from passing woe.

INACCESSIBLE

I saw one misty morning
An orchid on a tree,
And like a flute of silver
Its blossoms called to me.

The plaintive cry of beauty
That mid decay is born
I heard there standing breast-deep
In sparkling dews of dawn,

And longed to pluck those mauve sprays
(Too high, alas, for me!)
From the shadow-weaving branches
Of that old and moss-draped tree.

FRUSTRATION

Love finds no fulfilment,
Its bitter-sweet
Fragrance no flower — no path
Its blindly wandering feet.

Only shrivelled buds in
An empty tomb,
A vase for tears — a star
Extinguished by the gloom.

TRANSIENCE

The world is full of falling leaves,
Of wistful things that come and go –
Flights of swallows through the skies,
Footprints of starlings in the snow.

Only one day the Summer rose
Across our path her scent can fling;
Not long the Autumn lily blooms,
Not long the crocus of the Spring.

'THE ASHES OF ALL MY HEARTACHES...'

The ashes of all my heartaches,
The dust of a hundred dreams,
Are swept away in an instant
When forth one white peak gleams.

After long storm and struggle,
My heart with quietness fills
At the curve of this jade-green river,
The sweep of these dark blue hills.

LOVE'S AUSTERITY

How sweet is love's austerity,
How fiercely sweet, when it denies
My hands the bliss of touching thee,
The heaven of looking to mine eyes.

With no more sweets to seek and find
Love wanes as bright full moon above;
But this harsh abstinence shall grind
A finer point upon my love.

A point so fine, an aim so true,
Upon my passion shall there be,
That it will pierce like lightning through
The veiled heart of Reality.

'IT IS NOT LOVE THAT SEEKS TO BIND...'

It is not love that seeks to bind
Two bodies in a fierce embrace;
Nor love, true love, that dreams to find
The highest beauty in a face.

Love soars beyond the scathe of hands,
Outstrips a face, and is employed
Where it both sees and understands
A Beauty without form and void.

THE EVENING WALK

We walked where thick green bamboo groves
Point down their speary leaves,
Feeling the quietness of the hills,
The silence that is eve's.

The sun's last light, all flecked with gold,
Full on our path did lie,
And mountains piled up inky blue
Against a pale green sky.

How strange, that when night's first white star
Burned through the heavens wide,
My heart should be so lonely, though
My love walked at my side!

GOLDFISH

In the dim green stillness of the pool
There is a redness as of gold
Flashing among the dark brown weeds,
Glimmer on glimmer, bright but cold,
Of the black-finned goldfish beautiful
That breathe down there where the lotus breeds.

Deep in the ocean of my soul
Flickers an anguish red as fire,
Twining among my oozy thoughts,
Glimmer on glimmer of hot desire
Leaping and sparkling beyond control
In the darkness there where the heart contorts.

As the fish that rises for grub or fly
May be laid gasping-golden on sand-strewn shore,
And glimmer no more in the dim green dawn
Of waters where lily and lotus lie,
So the fierce red love that racks me sore
May be laid on the bank of the harsh world's scorn

If up to the surface it should swim
For the grub of words or the fly of phrase
From where like the glimmer of fish in shoal
Now through the dark brown weeds it plays
With a ruby redness, a faint fierce gleam
In the dark green depths of my inmost soul.

BAMBOO ORCHIDS

With slender rosy stem
And long green leaves thrust out
Pink orchids violet-lipped
Stand poised as though for dance
Upon the gnarled tree's fork.

So fairy-like, so frail,
With long green trailing leaves,
So like a butterfly
Each exquisite rare bloom,
We half expect to see
Them flutter and fly away.

YASHODHARA

After the Painting by W. S. Bagdatopulos

Though rained thy kisses on His hand
Beneath the soft faint light
Of golden lamps, thy Lord slept on
Through the rich violet night.

The crimson flowers that round thy bed
Were scattered heedlessly,
Lay flung, although so beautiful,
Forgotten there – like thee.

With watching and with longing tired
You slept at last upon
Your soft white breasts, and dreamed till dawn
Rose drear – and He was gone.

QUATRAIN

What a fantastic creature is the poet,
Who in his quiet secluded garden sits
Musing upon a flower, while any minute
An Atom Bomb may blow the world to bits!

THE SECRET

Roll on, roll on for ever,
Thou Wheel of Death and Birth –
Build up another Heaven,
Spread out another Earth,
Where men may reap the harvest
Of deeds done ill or well,
Scoop out a place of torment,
Hollow another Hell –
Lift to the heights or hurl me
Sheer down the steep abyss;
I shall not laugh for that,
I shall not weep for this.
Who knows this wondrous secret
Has naught to seek or shun:
That the pain of the Wheel of Death and Birth
And Nirvana's peace are one.

'MANY WERE THE FRIENDS...'

I.

Many were the friends who sought with eager hands to lay
   hold of me as I passed along the way;
But I have shaken them all off and come with lonely longing
   to the door of my Friend.
Many were the flowers that blossomed around me in the garden
   where I strayed;
But I have sought out the White Rose while it was still
   bright with morning dew.
Many were the instruments I heard playing in the symphony
   of life;
But I have cared to listen only to the melancholy sweetness
   of Thy flute beneath the stars.

II.

When the dawn wings like a great golden bird from the East,
In the cool of early morning, beside the pine trees,
I wait for Thee...
When the sun hangs poised like a red flamingo in the
   heavens,
In the quivering heat of noon, wrapped in the mauve-blue
   mist of the jacaranda,
I wait for Thee...
When the pale moon breasts the sky like a silver swan on a
   blue lake,
In the lone garden of my dreams, beneath the wide-
   spreading branches of the Tree of Life,
I wait for Thee...
While youth comes and goes, while manhood waxes and
   wanes as the moon,

In the midst of the world's tumult, and in the deep silence
    of my heart,
Through life and through death, through the birth and
    dissolution of millions of universes, eternally
I wait for Thee…

III.
When will He come?
When will the dust of my life blossom beneath the invincible
    ardour of His footsteps?
When will the ashes of my heart flame beneath the
    all-enkindling touch of His hands?
O listen! By day the tall grass whispers to the listless trees,
    When will He come?
And all night the jasmine murmurs to the stars, When will
    He come?
But day and night I make question of the heavens and the
    earth,
When will He come? When will He come? When will He
    come?

1951 LONGING

For the Boundless, the Unlimited, the Infinite I long.
Unfold the wings of my heart like the wings of a bird in song
At the midmost arch of the sky, in the full blue blaze of day,
When the ear can hear its note, though the eye tracks not its way.

For the height of the Beyondless, All-Transcending, do I yearn.
My heart's desire flames upward, as the red fires upward burn
From the earth's fierce fiery centre, through the cold grey crust that bars
Life's journey up the Milky Way, love's flight among the stars.

THE ROOT SPEAKS

Mock me not, O Rose, that I am hidden
Here in the black soil. The sap descends
In Autumn with the long tale of thy Summer beauty
And I know all thy ways. Oh mock me not
That my roots are hidden in the earth, that I love the earth
With its moist smell of rotting leaves and its decayedness.
Mock me not that my friends are all children of uncleanness
And my loves the daughters of earth. I have heard report
Of your pure white beauty bediamonded with drops of dew,
And of how you stand stately and aloof among your leaves
    and thorns.
The stars are all on fire for you,
And the moon maddened by your beauty.
Oh mock me not that I am ugly and twisted and black.
I am out of your sight. Why should you mock me?
But tell me, Whence comes the sap that invigorates your veins,
And the beauty that blushes in every petal?
Does it not come with the ascending sap in Spring?
Comes it not through these roots, from this dank black soil,
From these rotting leaves, this decayedness, this uncleanness –
Out of urine and ordure? So mock me not,
O Rose, nor be ashamed of your father the Root
Before the faces of your friends, the Stars.

'FORGIVE ME IF I HAVE STAINED...'

Forgive me if I have stained
Your beauty with my desire,
Or troubled your clear serene
Light with my fury of fire.
Forgive me; let us be friends.

Forgive me if I have looked
For response that you could not give,
Or raised in the deeps of my heart
This red rose too sickly to live.
Forgive me; let us be friends.

THE HEART'S NO

Brain says, Beauty will perish,
Flake on flake, like the snow,
Leave but a pool of wan water
That you may see and know
How grey you have grown with dreaming –
But still the heart sings 'No'.

Head says, loving is folly,
And only the cold are wise,
Who have sealed up Love's mouth of music,
Put out his burning eyes,
And turned him loose in the desert –
But the heart still 'No' replies.

LINES

I questioned, in my greener age,
Whether it were best for me
To blossom Poet or burgeon Sage;
But now in riper days I see,
And with what gladness know it:
The Poet is the truest Sage,
The Sage the sweetest Poet –
The piper his own best tune;
And laugh that I could ever
Have striven thus to sever
The moonlight from the moon.

MAITREYA

Lost in these yellowing Autumn woods, I see
A Buddha seated under every tree;
And each white peak, and each dark violet hill,
Seems a giant Buddha meditating still.
So poised this earth, so quiet its sky above,
They seem like Maitreya deep in thoughts of love.

PLATO'S REPLY

*'All dreams of the soul
End in a beautiful man's or woman's body.'*
W.B. YEATS

That is all very well...

But the bodies of your beautiful man and woman
Must one day grow old –
Yea, though they had walked about all their lives
With limbs of gold.
One day they must perish and then the dead are
Most grey and cold –
But not so cold and grey as the dreams that have
ended in them,
No, nor so old.

But if the beautiful man's or woman's body
End in a dream
Of Beauty Itself, the Shine behind the shadows
Of things that seem,
That perishing bodily beauty will the Eternal
Beauty redeem,
And keep it alive in the soul like a dream folded
Within a dream.

SONG

Tread softly as a cat
Uncoiling from the mat
In quest of prey;
For who treads soft goes far,
E'en to the Morning Star
And Milky Way.

But tread most softly when
You have to do with men
Of simple parts;
For, if truth were said,
All unawares you tread
Upon their hearts.

RHYMED HAIKU

Autumn clouds, like snow
In Summer, drift the way
    We all must go.

RHYMED HAIKU

Oh darkness is done
And snow-peaks catch crimson
    The smile of the sun!

RHYMED HAIKU

How still the mists lie
Growing deeper till hills are
    As blue as the sky!

RHYMED HAIKU

On the hillside wait
Clouds calm as my thoughts
   And as intimate.

RHYMED HAIKU

Dawn brightening
Across the sky like the unfolding of
   A sunbird's wing!

LUMBINI

I remember a pool of blue lotuses
Blooming at Lumbini near the dusty highroad,
And the miracle of those blue flowers rising
So purely from the black waters, told me
Far more of the birth of the Enlightened One
Than the broken Ashoka column, or ruined shrine.

ANIMIST

I feel like going on my knees
To this old mountain and these trees.
Three or four thousand years ago
I could have worshipped them, I know.
But if one did so in this age
They'd lock him in a padded cage.
We've made the world look mean and small
And lost the wonder of it all.

THE POET'S EYE

Though veil on veil of gleaming blue
Translucence o'er the hills is furled,
The poet's eye sinks through and through
Deep as the beauty of the world;

Deep as the Truth all men desire
He plumbs, and then his vision sings
With lightning glance that sets afire
The poetry of common things.

THE CHARCOAL-BURNERS

Once more the deep blue Winter skies
Dissolve in tenderest green;
Once more in purple shadow rise
The hills; once more is seen
Eve's first faint star; and lo, once more
The charcoal-burners pass my door.

First gnarled old men, then cheerful boys,
With young men in the pride
And blush of opening manhood's joys,
Plod up the mountain-side;
And after, sharing all they do,
Red-shawled, blue-skirted women too.

Up the long, winding mountain road,
With naked, sturdy limbs,
Each bears his black, dull-gleaming load,
Before the red light dims;
With broad, bowed backs, and labouring breath,
Like lost souls on the road to death.

The sweat-drops tell how far away
That world where fancy sees
The glooms wherein they heard all day
A noise of falling trees;
And saw, to charcoal slowly turning,
The beauty of the forest burning.

What tongue can tell, what happy flight
Of fancy e'er discover,
How many trees that loved the light
Were stricken from their lover;
How many forests filled with breath
Charred into hideousness and death.

Year after year, this mountain road
Remorseless will they tread,
Like death's own self, with ghastly load,
Till the forests are all dead;
Like man himself, that will not cease
Till he has ruined Nature's peace.

BUFFALOES BEING DRIVEN TO MARKET

We know when market-day is near,
For village folk to vend their store,
Because the blue-grey buffaloes
Are driven in the night before.

With long-lashed eyes, and massive horns
Low-curving from each patient head,
They shuffle sadly up the road,
Dusty, and lowing to be fed.

Their drivers, shouting from the rear,
Urge them with blows to left or right,
And, mindful of the broad red sun,
Make haste before the fall of night.

One evening, as I watched them pass,
My heart was heavy for their kind,
To see how slowly one great beast
Limped painfully along behind.

Slowly he moved, and slower yet,
Despite their whip and blood-stained goad,
Till, sagging at the knees, he dropped
On the sere grass beside the road.

He tossed his patient head; I saw
The deep blue eyes were glazed with pain.
Though shivering in a storm of blows
He could not rise and walk again.

And as the darkness fell, I mused
That simple folk who sell and buy
Could herd him to the butcher's shed,
Yet could not let him rest and die.

NO WORD

Some men can find no word for Love:
What Truth is, none could ever say.
But I, this day,
Though searching, for the beauty of
A bamboo by the breezes stirred
Can find no word.

QUATRAIN

Walking along the mountain paths,
A pink-white cloud I saw appear
Floating athwart the trees – the first
Wild cherry-blossom of the year.

'UP AND DOWN THE GRAVEL PATH...'

Up and down the gravel path,
Between the flowering trees,
I've walked this Summer afternoon
To give my spirit ease.

I could not idly stand, nor sit
Upon the grassy ground,
For like a mill-wheel in my head
The thoughts flew round and round.

Oh thoughts of life and thoughts of death
Chased thoughts of love and pain
Like golden hawk and sable dove
Inside my reeling brain.

The withered hopes like wind-whirled leaves
Thick on my heart did come,
With dreads like shapes that dance for blood
About the sorcerer's drum.

So up and down the shadowy paths,
Between the moon-white trees,
Through pools of silver, I must walk
To give my spirit ease.

TIBETAN TRUMPETS

Knit with my heart these trumpets seem
That deeply sound from hill to hill;
Booming through mist so mournfully,
Holding their note of pain, until
With its reverberation loud
The sympathetic valleys fill.

Groaning their sorrows out, all night
Far off the giant trumpets play;
But the deep thunder of their grief
Resounds within my heart all day –
Type of the anguish of mankind
Rolling among life's hills for aye.

HIEROGLYPHICS

Sun, moon, the mountains and the plain,
The silvered ocean's ceaseless roll,
With all four seasons in their round,
Are hieroglyphics of the soul.

And that is why yon Evening Star
Can script the secret of my breast,
And hang, an unshed burning tear,
On the wan visage of the West.

'I THINK THERE LIVES MORE WISDOM...'

I think there lives more wisdom
In what the poets write
Than all the scribbling fingers
Of sages could indite,
With doubt and speculation
Troubling the starry night.

I think there shines more charity
From wretched broken hut
Or hovel than from churches
And sects where hearts are shut,
Whose rule and motto seems to be
'We must love our neighbours — but...'

Therefore a poet
And a poor man will I be,
Loving my neighbour as myself,
Of wealth and wisdom free;
And from sages, sects and churches,
Good Lord, deliver me.

MAN'S WAY

The red rose does not whisper
'What loveliness is mine!'
Nor the sun upon his azure tower
Cry out 'Behold, I shine!'
Yet some poor mortal women,
By passion crazed or worse,
Can flaunt a rag of beauty
O'er half the universe;
And men no whit the better
Think that if they but frown
A cloud will darken heaven
And the stars come raining down.
Even the ragged goose-girl
Preens as her bare feet pass
By her face's muddied image
In the rain-filled rut, her glass;
While the young wretch, her brother,
Leaps toward her with a gun
And a dead crow, shouting joyfully
'Oh look what I have done!'

'IN THE WOODS ARE MANY MORE'

Selling wild orchids at my door one day
A man said, 'In the woods are many more...
Deep in the gloom, high on the thickset trees,
Wild orchids hang like clouds of butterflies,
Golden and white, spotted with red and black,
As huge as birds, or tiny as a bee,
Wild orchids which no eye has ever seen
Save ours, who wander in these rich green glooms
All day throughout the year.' I bought his sprays,
Paid him, and bore them in; and as I went
My eyes by chance fell on a shelf of books, –
The Buddha's Teachings, – and thereafter glanced
Up to the Buddha's image as He smiled
Above them from the alcove. Strange it was
That, as my eyes from book to image passed,
Dwelling an instant on that calm, pure Face,
There, with the frail cold blossoms in my hands,
The words that man spoke at my door should ring
Through my stilled heart again and yet again
Like music – 'In the woods are many more...'

SUMMER AFTERNOON

Now it is early summer, and the woods
Ring all day with the cuckoo's double cry;
The heat grows week by week, and from the blue
Intolerable heavens beats the sun
Fiercer and fiercer on the huge red flowers
That droop among the grasses; dragonflies
In their bright sapphire mail hang glitteringly
Upon the fountain's edge, four gauze wings poised
For instant flight. At peace amid the sights
And sounds of nature, with a drowsy cat
Limp on my knee, and an unheeded book
Of poems slipping down into my lap
Unread, I dream away the quiet hours.

AWAKENING

Often do I remember the huge untidy nests
Of peacocks on the Ganges' silver shore,
Built in the forks of gnarled and stunted trees
Among the red flowers of the oleander;
Often remember with what beauty streamed
The long tail feathers of the sitting bird
Over the edge, and almost to the ground;
Often remember all those moonlit nights,
When swifter than a dream the river fled,
Riddled with silver, through its ghostly banks,
While in the heaven of heavens above us marched
Bright squadrons of innumerable stars;
Often remember the coming of the dawn,
The first faint silver in the east, the glow
Of rose-gold light among the pale green trees,
The coolness, and the stir of things from sleep;
Often remember, through my dreams, that world
Of beauty shattered by a peacock's raucous cry.

HAIKU

White clouds on the hills
Linger a while, then vanish
　In the blue distance.

HAIKU

Waterfalls from stone
To mossy stone trickling
　Down deep cool ravines.

LINES

Men think that they have understood,
When, at some rose or butterfly
Which they have sighted in a wood,
They fling some gross latinity.
O empty heads, O hearts in folly old,
To dream the truth of things could thus be told!

MANIFESTO*

I'll write my poems for my friends,
For those who love me. Why to waste
Long hours in studying schools and trends,
For what would suit the public's taste?

These rocks shall be my publisher;
I'll raise a column in the sun,
And, like Ashoke, that faith aver,
Which made my heart's torn empire one.

Or else, when other Muse conceives,
I'll scatter, subtly Sibylline,
My love upon the forest leaves,
On every leaf one burning line.

THE SURVIVOR

The loose red earth is washed away,
At once the storm-swept hills are bare;
Gaunt trees fall crashing down the slopes,
And sodden leaves stick everywhere.

Day after day the rains drummed down,
Nor sturdiest growth could meet the shock,
Save one frail bush, with scarlet flowers,
Whose root had pierced the stubborn rock.

A RAINY DAY IN THE MOUNTAINS

The rain has been falling all day; the maize-fields are sodden and brown;
The green lush growth of the garden is matted and beaten down;
The hills round their bare blue shoulders draw closer their mantles grey,
And the sun gleams through like a pearl, but so faintly it scarce seems day.

Yet the road that winds up from the valley is thronged with market-folk;
White bulls draw the creaking waggons, lurching beneath the yoke;
With wet brown limbs plod the coolies, bearing their loads from the plain,
While the women hurry behind them, red-shawled from the streaming rain.

I have watched all day at the window, while strange thoughts came and went
As I mused on the life of the mountains, wherewith mine own seems blent;
And I glimpsed through the rain-dark heavens a cloudless Autumn sky,
While the mists round the mountains' loins hid no secret from mine eye.

Deeper the life of the mountains, oh richer and grander far,
Than the huddled life of the cities, where the mushroom hovels are,
Where no change of tint in Autumn, no show of leaf in Spring,
Brightens the dusty wayside trees where bird ne'er hops to sing.

But the cheerless day is ending, and the rains have almost done;
Creeps with the lengthening shadows a redness round the sun;
With eve-gilt limbs, with baskets of charcoal, rice and corn,
In the shadow of the mountains plod on the mountain-born.

THE ABOMINABLE SNOWMAN

I.
Where the ice glitters, where untrodden snows
Stretch soft and soundless, where a frore wind blows,
The Abominable Snowman comes and goes.

Oft the lone mountaineer, through a swarm
Of snowflakes whose white dance presages storm,
Has glimpsed the naked giant's fearful form.

While oft the hermit, solitary quite,
Has heard him howling all a Winter's night,
And tow'rd the monster winged a shaft of Light.

But whether these be tales or no, by day –
A thing of dread for all who pass that way,
Deep in the snow the giant Footprints splay.

II.
Appear, as soon as newspapers are able
To send reporters, photos of the fable;
And hot words flow at many a breakfast-table.

Pundits in London, Paris and Berlin
Let loose at once a loud but learned din,
All arguing, not for Truth, but just to win.

'I'm sure there must have been a bear about!'
'Nonsense, a monkey's paw, without a doubt!'
'A human footprint by the wind splayed out!'

Pamphlets fly back and forth, as Doctor D.
Refutes Professor M., though all agree
A Snowman's footprint it could *never* be.

III.
Yet still, despite a hundred learned Noes,
O'er shining glaciers, through unruffled snows,
The legendary Creature comes and goes.

But even if one day the truth came out
That it was ape or bear they'd fussed about
I should not think my faith had suffered rout.

Nor could I share the gleeful scholar's pride
That, thanks to Science, another myth had died,
And one more fact been neatly classified.

Rather than one of that all-knowing band
I'd be a Sherpa or Tibetan, and
Believe there are some things we *don't* understand.

RECIPROCITY

The surest way of gaining is to give.
To learn a secret, tell one of your own.
How often lovers, wishing to find out
If the beloved loved or not, have said
'I love you', waiting what seemed endless minutes
To hear those three words echoed back again.
Loving means giving, just as dawn means day,
So that to say 'I love', means 'I will give',
And to find out if the beloved loves
Means to find out if he or she will give
What we desire to have. This subtle key
Unlocks full many a time life's fast-closed doors.
Poet or painter gazes at a flower,
Mountain or stream, or any living form,
Until he falls in love with it, and gains
Its heart by the surrender of his own, –
Till he can re-create, not what he saw,
But that which he experienced and became.
Giving his heart to Truth, the devotee
Wins in return the sacred heart of Truth,
And keeping nothing for himself, gains all.
Selfish and secretive can ne'er believe
The surest way of gaining is to give,
Nor learn life's secret, holding fast their own.

TRANSFORMATION

No fruit without the seed. Desire
Has flowered into a star tonight.
By subtle alchemies my fire
Turns heatless, and shines forth as light.

From link to link th' enchainment grows
That each to all and all to each
Doth bind, – the ordure to the rose;
Height mates with Depth, while thought to speech

Leaps as a lover to his love.
Oh fools who strive to separate
Below from the embraces of Above,

Wisdom from Beauty, if the seed's destroyed
Where are the flowers that ye would consecrate?
Ye know not the great mystery of the Void.

TAKING REFUGE IN THE BUDDHA

Natthi me saranam annam
Buddho me saranam varam

Not where the gardens blossom;
Not where the fountains rise
In plumes of trembling whiteness
To the blue of sunlit skies;
Not where the forests murmur;
Not where the rivers meet;
Not where the mountains ponder:
— My place is at Thy Feet.

Not where the spring Castalian
Spreads glimmering as it gropes
Through the ever-living laurels
That throng Parnassus' slopes;
Not where the Nine still follow
With dance and chorus sweet
In the footsteps of Apollo:
— My place is at Thy Feet.

Not where the armies muster;
Not where the trumpet calls
To the legions as they glitter
Beneath beleaguered walls;
Not where the vultures gather;
Not where the ravens eat;
Not where the nations wrangle:
— My place is at Thy Feet.

Not in the preacher's pulpit;
Not in the scholar's chair;
Not where the lawyer chambers
With lies and musty air;
Not on the throne of judgement;
Not in the scorner's seat;
Not at the merchant's counter:
—My place is at Thy Feet.

Not where the gaunt Cross rises;
Not where the Crescent shines
Like a drawn blade in the heavens;
Not where the Gopi pines;
Not where the organ thunders;
Not where the tom-toms beat;
Not where the conch is wailing:
—My place is at Thy Feet.

Not where the gold spire flashes
Against blue sun-drenched skies;
Not where the vestments dazzle;
Not where the prayers arise;
Not where the incense thickens;
Not where the priests repeat
Dead words they do not understand:
—My place is at Thy Feet.

Not in Nirvana's stillness;
Not in Samsara's flow;
Not in the heavens above us;
Not in the hells below;
Not in thought or word or action;
Not where mind and object meet:
 —With Wisdom and Compassion
My place is at Thy Feet.

LOOKING AT THE MOON ON A FROSTY NIGHT

The moon is cold and hard and small
And glitters like a crystal ball;
The trees are steeped in silver light: —
Ah, what a clear-cold winter's night!

WINTER IN THE HILLS

The icy wind has planted
Fresh roses in your cheek;
Your voice rings clear and joyous
Through the cold air as we speak.

By day the sky is bluer,
By night the fire more red;
For coldness brings out colours
That heat could ne'er have bred.

Between the leafless branches
The landscape is ablaze
With green and gold and scarlet
All the short bright winter days.

When youth and beauty vanish,
And death impends above,
May age but make more vivid
The colours of our love.

ARGOSIES

A solitary boy would sail his boat
All day in a green pool, where willows wept
Over the stony verge, and sadly trailed
Their slim green leaves along the water's face.
Only the bright-eyed ducks with blue-barred wings,
And small black waterfowl with scarlet eyes,
Saw him, as, racing half way round the pool,
With eager eyes he waited for his joy
To steer towards him from the other side.
Oh how like a white swan it seemed to cut
Through the clear water, tilting as the breeze
Leaned on the silver sails, until it dipped, –
So gracefully, – one white wing in the waves!
Now like a crescent moon its sharp prow cleaves
The cloudy shallows, where dead yellow leaves
And floating sticks impede its passage, and
It drifts into the small exultant hands
Outstretched towards it. With what ecstasy
Did that boy, more than twenty years ago,
Sail his white boat on that green pool! – Oh why?
Was to his infant soul obscurely given,
Beneath the brown shade of the willow trees,
Foreknowledge of those argosies which now
Loom white-winged o'er him from the deeps of life?

THE TREE OF WISDOM

A Poem for Wesak

All pleasures of all sense; the fickle mind's
Delight in idle thought; attachment strong
To child and wife, to pomp and luxury
And empire, dropped away like withered husks,
Till only a naked love for all mankind
Was left Him, as a heart within His heart.
This love He scattered seedlike on the rocks
Of penance, where the thorny cactus grew
Sere in the blistering sun; but all He reaped
In that harsh field was pain, while through a mist
As though of blood He saw around Him men
Whose arms, stretched motionless above their heads,
Were like the dead boughs of a withered tree
Blasted by lightning; others in the midst
Of four bright fires, the sun in heaven for fifth,
Squatting in filth and nakedness He saw;
While smeared with dust and ashes others crouched
Beastlike at roots of trees, or hung like bats
Head downward from the branches, or like dogs
Ravened on ordure, hoping thus (vain hope!)
To conquer heav'n, or stay their minds on peace.
Then darkness fell, and ringing in His ears
A voice came, like a peal of jangling bells
Clanging out doubts, and then a silence, till
After He knew not how long nothingness,
The trickle of warm milk between His lips
As the goat straddled, and the neatherd pressed
The new life drop by drop into His own,

So that the loveseed nestling in His heart
Swelled quickening. Then with joy He cast it down
Like a wise sower on the fertile soil
Of perfect meditation. All night long
He watched the germ burst and the young shoot climb
Up higher; the stem thicken; branches spread
More plenteously, twigs finelier, broad green leaves
Denser and darker; while the Wesak Moon
Climbed with the climbing tendrils till she stood
High in the heav'ns, and poured her silver light
Wave after wave upon the full-grown Tree
Of Wisdom, as it towered between the earth
And heavens in one white and dazzling sheet
Of radiance, glittering gem-like as it moved.
Thenceforward through a score of centuries,
That men beneath its far-flung shade might rest,
Unshakeably it stood. Love from its boughs
Dropped seedlike, and a family of Trees
Of Wisdom overshadowed half the world.
Then from the West moaned thunder, and a storm
Blackened the sky with clouds that, rolling thick
In the meridian, round its stately crown
Flung furious bolts as the bright levin-flash
In crescents and in crosses struck the Tree
Time and again, while the fanátic winds
Howled round the pillared trunk and, tugging, strove
To drag its ancient boughs down, or pluck out
Those roots that through a hundred thousand lives
Mined dragonwise, and coiled round mighty stones
Far in the depths of being. But the Tree
Firm as the ponderous axle of the world
Stood until morning, with its family

Of trees, though somewhat shorn of leaves, with here
A rotten branch down, there a sapling split,
Fronting the clear sky like a giant refreshed
By dreams of battle. Oh drop down again,
O seed of love, upon the storm-scarred earth,
Drop richly from those fruitful boughs, and plant
Fresh families more thick and tall and fair
Than she has known before, that all her graves
May turn to greenness, all her blood to beauty.
Plant every valley, every hillside slope
And bouldered mountain; plant the yellow sands;
Plant the five continents to their coasts, until
The seas are overarched, the ocean spanned
With many-pillared leafage, and the Trees
Of Wisdom, overshadowing all the world,
Spread wide and deep and cool their shade, that man
May rest beneath them, even as the Lord
Beneath His Tree on that first Wesak Morn
Rested, and knew that the long quest was done!

CERTAINTIES

The wisest doubt if Truth
Be true indeed;
But that a rose is beautiful
The world's agreed.

Whether we hold or not
Life ends in death,
That love's most bitter-sweet
Who questioneth?

Based not on dreams, but on
His certainty
Of beauty, love and pain
Man's life must be.

THE MODERN BARD

We cannot sing as Orpheus wist
To sing upon the hills of Thrace
When the beloved, serpent-kissed
To death, is snatched from our embrace.

Profounder hells than Orpheus knew
We've plumbed, and yet we cannot sing
Persephone and Dis so true,
So sweet, so wonderful a thing

As Orpheus sang in those dim halls,
By that still stream, with eager breath;
'Twixt our Inferno's brick-built walls
Love never triumphed over death.

And even when we've stumbled out,
Too sick for mirth, and have been torn
In pieces by the wild-beast rout
And man and music wildly borne

Down some swift river's flow, and flung
Headlong into the sounding sea,
Our lyre, though it had oft-times sung
Her name, calls not 'Eurydice!'

MADRIGAL

Red as roses blushing,
White as lilies paling,
Hot as Summer flushing,
Cold as Winter failing –
Love is like all weather,
Everything together.

Hoping and despairing,
Singing loud and sighing,
Smiles and frowns both wearing,
Living and yet dying –
In Love's bitter-sweet
All extremes do meet.

THE PIONEER

Since that his eyes were like two wells
Wherein black waters sparkle deep
They thought him well-nigh dead, and said
His spirit could no longer keep
Firm hold of its exhausted frame,
More than on burnt-up sticks a flame.

Later, his eyes were like two stars
Glimmering at eve through dewy air
(Sujáta's gift had wrought the change),
And then they murmured one so fair
Enlightenment could hardly gain
Through comfort, who had failed through pain.

But when his eyelids drooped, half closed
At dawn, on sun-surpassing eyes,
They knew whate'er they'd thought or said
Had been to him but as the cries
Of weak-eyed bats that flit about
At evening ere the moon is out.

For one whose undimmed eye sees Truth
Like sunlight on a distant hill
Mindful of that alone must fare,
Deaf and blind to all else, until
Dawns in his face, grief's long night spent,
The sun-smile of enlightenment.

THE CONQUEST OF MARA

Whether within his mind dark forces rolled
Wavelike along, and dashed their bitter spume
At his enlightened dawn-skies' blue and gold;
Or whether, like a bank of clouds that loom

On the horizon's verge, presaging storm,
Black Mara and his host embattled came
With many a fearful face and hideous form,
On monsters mounted, panoplied in flame,

I know not. Fact or symbol, all I know,
Or care to know, is that the arrowy showers,
The hard-flung spears and javelins of the foe,
Touching his halo's edge, were turned to flowers

That rained all night beneath the Bodhi Tree
As though in adoration, or as though
In homage to his súpreme victory...

Flowers of the earth or thought-flowers, all I know
Is that Compassion, sunlike, can transmute
Our hate not only into flowers, but fruit.

EPITAPH ON KRISHNA, PRINCESS IRENE'S SQUIRREL

Now he's gone, the best of squirrels,
Not ev'n his mistress can entice
His happy spirit to her shoulder
From the trees of Paradise.

SONNET

Oh Death himself was Orpheus' audience!
And Death's pale consort, on her ivory throne,
Could weep as though her heart was not a stone
As the song breathed into her buried sense
The fields of Enna and lost innocence,
And love lost, and the lyrist singing lone
Sadder and sweeter than the earth had known.
Rough beasts themselves were then his audience.

But we, tired lyrists of a tuneless age,
Soothe not the ear of Death in shadowy grot.
Death's consort sits unmoved the whole night long.
Uncharmed the red-pawed wolf and leopard rage.
Oh what to speak of Death! Life hears us not!
Or brutes, when men themselves are deaf to song!

SONNET

The thunders rolled beneath me, as I sate
On Truth's most high, cold mountain-peak alone,
Secure within the 'intellectual throne',
Ruling Thought's kingdom with Olympian state;
Open upon my knees the Book of Fate
Rattled its iron leaves madly, tempest-blown,
While, from the dim horizons of the known
I lifted up mine eyes to contemplate

The unknown Void beyond. Oh bright as dawn
The Heaven of Beauty shining there afar
I saw, and rose as wild with love and joy
As Zeus did, when his sleepless lids one morn
Saw far below him, like a fallen star,
The beauty of the fair Bithynian boy.

THE BODHISATTVA'S REPLY

What will you say to those
Whose lives spring up between
Custom and circumstance
As weeds between wet stones,
Whose lives corruptly flower
Warped from the beautiful,
Refuse and sediment
Their means of sustenance —
What will you say to them?

That woman, night after night,
Must sell her body for bread;
This boy with the well-oiled hair
And the innocence dead in his face
Must lubricate the obscene
Bodies of gross old men;
And both must be merry all day,
For thinking would make them mad —
What will you say to them?

Those dull-eyed men must tend
Machines till they become
Machines, or till they are
Cogs in the giant wheel
Of industry, producing
The clothes that they cannot wear
And the cellophaned luxury goods
They can never hope to buy —
What will you say to them?

Or these dim shadows which
Through the pale gold tropic dawn
From the outcaste village flit
Balancing on their heads
Baskets to bear away
Garbage and excrement,
Hugging the wall for fear
Of the scorn of their fellow-men –
What will you say to them?

And wasted lives that litter
The streets of modern cities,
Souls like butt-ends tossed
In the gutter and trampled on,
Human refuse dumped
At the crossroads where civilization
And civilization meet
To breed the unbeautiful –
What will you say to them?

'I shall say nothing, but only
Fold in Compassion's arms
Their frailty till it becomes
Strong with my strength, their limbs
Bright with my beauty, their souls
With my wisdom luminous, or
Till I have become like them
A seed between wet stones
Of custom and circumstance.'

IMMENSITIES

Round this boundless universe's
Unseen axle, night and day,
Roll in clouds the bright star-clusters
Billion trillion miles away —

Wheel the great galactic systems
Whose immensities appal;
But the Wisdom of the Buddha
Has plumbed and measured all.

Spinning round this dire becoming's
Nave of ignorance, desire
And hate, our lives whirl madly
Like sparks of crimson fire —

Scarlet rings of pain and anguish
That to gods and men befall;
But the Buddha's great Compassion
Has embraced and conquered all.

ON A POLITICAL PROCESSION

Calcutta, 1953

Red-bannered hatred fills the streets
And flows from square to square,
Gathering as though in pools of blood
Around the rostrum, where
A speaker hoisted from the van
Upholds the Brotherhood of Man.

CALCUTTA

How can wracked soul and ruined body pass
Their days in this grey city, year by year?
Street after street without a blade of grass!
Face upon face and not a smile or tear!

NAGARJUNIKONDA*

Lines written on hearing that, under a scheme for the irrigation of the area, the ancient Buddhist site of Nagarjunikonda, so intimately associated with the career of the greatest Mahayana sage, was threatened with submergence

Where hills humped, there must be
The swirl and swish of the sea
We know. But oh must man
Inaugurate Nature's plan
Before the crumbling age
Confounds in dotard rage
Solid and liquid mass?
(Continents change and pass!)
With Titan force, need he
Stretch river into sea
And bury these green graves
Of faith, far under waves?
The gaunt-framed people grow
Spectrally thin: we know
That hunger's filled and fed
Not with carved stones, but bread.
Yet (not against thy voice,
Compassion, nor by choice)
Culture drops tears and pleads
For toppled shrines in weeds
Clad, and sad sculptured stone, –
Little she has to call her own, –
And to Pity cries for pity
On Nagárjun's city,
On the ruined roofs of the wise, where

Iron wall, gold stair
Flashed sheer in the sun. Oh let
Wisdom, Compassion's dam, be honoured yet,
And, like long buried seed,
In earth-womb stir, leap, breed,
Till branched o'er Deccan plain
Broods the Dragon Tree again.

THE VASE OF MOONLIGHT   *1954*

Your beauty, in repose, is like a vase
Of jasper or white jade with moonlight filled;
Your smiling is as though the moonlight spilled;
Your laugh, its shivering into a thousand stars.

A movement is as though the jewels within
Had fountained, or run sparkling like a stream;
Your sleeping is as though the heavenly gleam
Had found a soft white cloud to harbour in.

Your loving is as though the moonlight poured
In one bright stream from your vase into mine,
Whose earthen lip dare greet not crystal thine;
Your faithfulness is moonlight sealed and stored.

But melancholy makes you sapphirine,
O Vase of all my joys, and endless yearning
As though it were an evening sky is turning
Your moonlight into palest, purest green.

THE STREAM OF STARS

The stream of my desire no more
Rolls through the muddy fields of earth;
Between the azure banks of heaven
A stream of stars has come to birth.

No more on my soul's current float
Dead leaves from wind-dishevelled trees;
But swanlike, many a shining boat
Bends low before the heavenly breeze.

The fountains of my heart no more
Ooze slow into some stagnant place,
But in great tranquil rivers pour
Into the boundless sea of space.

NOCTURNE

Calcutta, 1954

Grey sleepers, wrapped in noisome rags,
Lay stretched out on the paving stones
As through the silence of the streets
We walked, and talked in quiet tones.

Against black walls belatedly
Old beggars crouched with rusty tins;
Rummaged the famished dogs and cats
Through overflowing garbage bins.

Sometimes a taxi, creeping past,
Purred to us of debauch's lair,
While blue and red the neon lights
Burned through the smoke-filled city air.

Our theme was friendship, beauty, art…
And as we thrid those streets, despite
Their squalor, in the moon, all round
We saw the beauty of the night.

JOY IN FLIGHT

How like a bird it comes and goes,
This joy, this sudden rapt ascension
Where knowledge pure as nectar flows
Beyond all earthly apprehension;

How like an eagle, whose descent
At noon upon the sleepy fold
Is as though wrath Olympian sent
A thunderbolt new-fledged with gold;

How like a gull, whose lonely flight
Must span a thousand leagues of foam
And breaking billows infinite
Before it ends in rest and home;

How like —when thought and image fail
As clouds wind-scattered from the moon—
The glorious unseen nightingale
That sings in leafy woods of June!

THE GREAT WORK

With grey-green fir and blue-black pine communing,
With tulip-tree and smooth camellia, — where
The last dark red and first white rose are blooming,
I sit, reclining in my cane armchair.

Head propped on hand, from dawn to dusk the garden,
Through sparse leaves peering with a thousand eyes,
Beholds me as I watch the sunbeams harden
And eve drip coldly from the wintry skies.

Day after day, beside my friend the mountain
I sit, and as in dream hear close at hand
My neighbours, tall bamboo and bubbling fountain,
Talking in words that I half understand.

Not indolence or ennui, soul-destroyers,
Nor sickness convalescent, holds me here,
But the Great Work, which to all mere enjoyers
Of 'doing' must as idleness appear.

But if against the sun you ever lifted
Red wine or emerald water in a bowl,
You'll know, recalling how their dregs were sifted,
I clear the turbid liquid of my soul.

And since in those dark waters still is lying
Thick sediment uncleared, so many days
Musing I sit, till, slowly purifying,
Shine through them as through crystal the sun's rays.

LINES

Between the mountain-crest and valley hung
A rainbow fragment, yellow, red and blue,
The iridescent child of light and rain,
And as I saw it from the height above
It seemed a symbol of my life, which gleams
Half way between the heavens and the earth
Rich with the rose of friendship, blue of art,
And glorious yellow of religious lore –
A rainbow fragment that one moment shines
And then dissolves in natal light and rain,
Until, as I believe, a purer heaven
Sees its unbroken circle shine serene.

ELUSIVE BEAUTY*

Well might the Poet question
Goddess Beauty, if she keeps
Her high state in heavenly mansions
Or in the infernal deeps –
Well his heart, perplexed, grow doubtful
As he worships at her shrine
If the Power which overshadows
Be demoniac or divine.

Thousand-eyed, to see our sorrows,
Thousand-armed, for succouring grace,
The Lord of Boundless Mercy
Looks down on every place;
But Beauty's forms protean
Have hands and feet and eyes
From the carrion by the wayside
To the moon in cloudless skies.

At times she haunts the forest,
Dryad-like, with naked feet;
Sometimes stumps an old blind beggar
Down a modern city street;
We see her in our sorrows
No less bright than in our joys –
In the smile beatific of the Buddha,
And the mischievous faces of boys.

Elusive as the shadows
That on windy days we see
Racing up and down the smooth white bole
Of the eucalyptus tree,
Beauty flies, and we must follow
Till she grant at last her kiss,
Caring not, so that be given,
Be it to Heaven or the Abyss.

EPIGRAM

We who have seen men murdered,
We who have seen bombs fall,
Muse not that Beauty passes
But that she stays at all.

A CRUMB FROM THE SYMPOSIUM

Believe not what you have heard
That love is a blazing fire:
Desire's not always love,
True love is never desire.
A reveller reeling
From Plato's feast
Has cried to the Morning Star
High in the East:
Let the torch burn on:
We shall waken at morn
To loves colder and purer
Than snows or the dawn.

STANZAS

Here, through the deep dark valley,
There, o'er the snow-peaks high,
Flows the turquoise green of water,
Towers the turquoise blue of sky.

As the eye tracks, so the heart treks
Earth below and heaven above –
Plunges deep to seek out wisdom,
Soars on high in quest of love.

KALINGA*

The third day of the slaughter saw a change;
The King no longer in his peacock tent
Cried 'Victory! Boundless now mine empire's range!'
He asked no longer how the death-roll went.

Head deep in hands, in that red dawn he sate
As stricken, and in fearful vision saw
The blackened land, the people's piteous fate,
Heaped slain, and all the ghastliness of war.

Lifting his eyes, grown sick of bloody sights,
And weary of the bloated face of Death,
He saw what gave him, after many nights
Of unquiet slumber, a more peaceful breath:

Instead of a red disc, it seemed there rolled
Across the heavens an eight-spoked Wheel of Gold.

DEFIANCE

Yet shall my soul burn upward like a fire.
Torment and sickness, penury and pain,
Shall be but as fresh fuel heaped amain
That makes the licking flame-tongues leap up higher.
Winged as an eagle shall my soul aspire
And, soaring sunlike in the sun's domain,
Scream loud defiance to the distant plain
Where creep the dull slow rivers of desire.

Or, if the flame múst sink, my soul shall burn
In red denial underneath the white
Ash of the world, and warm the grating-bars;
Or else, an eagle wearied, it shall spurn
All but the iciest crag, and brood all night
With no companion save the wind and stars.

THE QUEST

He could not find it with his wife and child,
Nor yet beneath dark-fronded forest boughs
Where peaceful hermits grazed their placid cows
Round quiet hermitage in pastures mild;
Something they lacked, though living undefiled
By aught sublunar; bright their anchorite brows
With prescience wreathed, and yet, for all their vows,
That which He sought He found not in the wild.

Six years of penance till His eyes were dim,
And shrivelled skin clung round the brittle bone,
Wondering the Band of Five saw then befall:
He found it not with them, nor they with Him.
But when they left Him He fared on alone,
And in that loneliness He found the All.

SONNET

To Him Who on that night of sleeping flowers
Left father, mother, child, wife – everything,
And went forth from His Palace of the Spring,
Forth from the hushed zenána's inmost bowers, –
Wherein, delighting and delighted, hours
He'd passed while smooth musicians strummed the string
And sang, – into the moonlight wandering,
Be praise from men, and from the heavenly powers!

Praise, that He left the pleasantness of love,
And praise, that He renounced the path of pain;
Praise, for those nights in meditation spent
Beneath the Tree, and praise, all praise above,
That in compassion, for our bliss and gain,
He could give up His 'own' Enlightenment.

QUATRAIN

Evening. Unstirred the western cloudlets lie
Like russet leaves in a blue lake of sky.
And in between them, silently and soon,
A gilded pinnace, glides the crescent moon.

RHYMED HAIKU

After three months rain
In a million drops the sun
Shines out again.

POSSIBILITIES　　　　　　　　　　　　　　　　*1956*

Our heart's a shapeless clay-lump
Whence by degrees we mould
Or Shiva's phallic emblem
Or Buddha bright with gold.

Our heart's a heap of tinder
Behind life's brazier-bars
Passion-consumed, or burning
With the ecstasy of the stars.

NALANDA REVISITED

Think not, my friends, that piling stone on stone,
Or laying brick on brick, as now we must
In this degenerate age, shall from the dust
Raise up those glories which were overthrown
When, like autumnal floods, from icy zone
Islam rolled down. Oh do not too much trust
Arches that ruinate and gates that rust
To guard the Buddha's treasure for His own!

Within our minds must Nalanda arise
Before we draw up plans, or measure ground:
If the foundation on our thoughts we lay,
Calm meditation, contemplation wise,
Above mundane vicissitudes shall found
A Nalanda that cannot pass away.

TO MANJUSHRI*

Lord of the Lotus, Flaming Sword, and Book,
Eternal Wisdom, Ever-Youthful One,
Dispeller of Illusion — as the sun
Packs off the clouds — with single radiant look, —
O Prince, whose pure compassion undertook
Freely, when Land-of-Snows was overrun
With evils, and the Good Law nigh undone,
Rebirth as him whose keen mind could not brook
Impurity or error, — yet once more
Descend! In this cold heart set up Thy state!
Give me Thy Lotus, spiritual rebirth;
Give me Thy Flaming Sword, that I may score
Vict'ry o'er those who darkly congregate
Against Thy Book, and drive them from the earth!

HOPE

Your sadness is my sadness, friend, and so
When yesterday I saw you, wan with grief,
I yearned to give some comfort or relief,
And thus it was, the reason of your woe,
Not merely curiously, I sought to know:
Your lofty tree of sorrows, leaf by leaf
You shed upon my breast, until in brief
Space you had covered it; naught else could grow.

What solace could I give? Yet, sipping tea
And darkly brooding o'er the future years
Half an hour later, – blessed with gleams of mirth
And friendship strengthened, – did we then not see
Shine through sun, rain, like Hope through smiles and tears,
The sev'n-hued rainbow spanning Heav'n and Earth?

THE VOICE OF SILENCE

Close, eyes; behold no more the rich array
Of forms and vivid colours. Touch, be still;
Grope not for lover's hand, or lips that will
Sting you awake to bliss by night or day.
Relish no more the scent of new-mown hay,
Or flowers, or incense, nostrils. Take your fill
Of tastes no more, O watery tongue, nor trill
Delicious notes in cadence grave or gay.

For when the senses and the sensual mind
Are laid asleep, and self itself suspended,
And naught is left to strive for or to seek,
Then, to the inmost spirit, thrice refined,
Thrice pure, before that trance sublime has ended,
With voice of thunder, will the Silence speak.

MEMORY

More than ten years ago, old Father Thames,
I saw your sluggish waters greyly glide
Washing th'Embankment on the northern side,
And on the southern lapping sodden stems
Of reeds with mud-encrusted diadems
Round crumbling steps, while up and down did ride
Trim launches, broad flat barges dignified
Piled high with huge, dull-gleaming sable gems.

More than ten years ago! Oh then it was,
Upon Westminster Bridge without a word
We stood, and saw below bright-glittering bars
Of moonlight on black water, – happy because
We were together, – and at midnight heard
How solemnly Big Ben spoke to the stars.

QUATRAIN

I saw two men, who nailed upon a cross
A third, high on a hill, outside a town;
All three I knew: one wore a crown of thorns,
A Homberg one, and one a triple crown.

SONNET

Flowers, that turn their faces to the sun,
And mighty forest trees, which seem to rise,
In Autumn, like a music to the skies,
Majestically green when day is done;
Fountains that laugh in gardens, every one;
Snowpeaks, half way to Heaven, that despise
Even the rosy kisses of sunrise;
Fire, mist, white clouds, and exhalations dun, –
All these, with man's own works, – as Gothic spire
And steeple, poised and tapering minaret,
Domed stupas, ruined but majestic yet
Above tree-tops, – in universal choir
Sing out above our mortal fume and fret,
With pealing organ voice, 'O Man, aspire!'

QUATRAIN

When Inspiration cracks the moulds of verse
The Poetry is not one whit the worse;
But when mere Theory, with hammer blows
Smashes – the result's not even prose.

SONNET

Work out the secret of your blood. The bright
Red drops into a ruby rosary string;
Tell on Desire's beads, importuning
With silk-smooth touch, the mantra of Delight;
Black is not always black, nor white aye white:
Yon snows, round whose purpúreal bases cling
The close-packed clouds, such colour-changes ring –
Now grey, now golden in the morning's light.

Dream not, therefore, that reddest need blush red
For ever, but as heavenliest nenuphar
From dunghill blooms, learn to distil, my son,
Wisdom divine from earth's rank lustihead,
Knowing that sunset shrouds the Evening Star,
And your life's secret and your blood's are one.

SONNET

Reading some books, you'd think the Buddha-Way,
As though macadamized, ran smooth and white,
Straight as an arrow, bill-boards left and right,
And that the yellow buses, thrice a day,
Whirled past the milestones, whose smug faces say,
'Nirvana 15 miles ... By 10 tonight
You'll all be there, good people, and alight
Outside the Peace Hotel, where you're to stay.'

But those who read their own hearts, inly wise,
Know that the Way's a hacked path, roughly made
Through densest jungle, deep in the Unknown…
And that, though burn a thousand baleful eyes
Like death-lamps round, serene and unafraid,
Man through the hideous dark must plunge alone.

THE CULT OF THE YOUNG HERO

Written after reading Stefan George

Do we not love the dawn, when first
Its faint streaks thread the eastern sky,
And snow peaks, greyly shadowed forth,
Flush rose and golden by and by?

Do we not love the new moon, when,
Like a young child, from cloudy bars
Released, it fingers wonderingly
The bright pure faces of the stars?

Then wherefore should we not, set free
From man's injurious hate and scorn,
Love, in the very eye of noon,

This boyish immaturity –
This beauty in its bud, its dawn,
And at the first phase of its moon?

LIFE AND DEATH

To J.E.C. and I.B.H.

Against a sky of purest turquoise rayed
The five symbolic hues, as from a sun,
While in the midst thereof sat, unafraid,
The Lord Chenrezi, the Compassionate One.

One pair of hands in taper fingers pressed
A lotus white and pearly rosary;
The other, palm to palm upon his breast,
Displayed the gesture of tranquillity.

Below, a ghastly skull, from which outcurving –
Black and obscene – two spiderish arms I saw,
With huge claw hands and talons vulturine,

Which, never from their evil purpose swerving,
A mangled human heart and cup of gore
Clutched, as the monstrous Female shrieked out 'Mine!'

STANZAS

From tone to tone of azure
The landscapes round me rise:
Blue-black are the valleys,
Ethereal blue the skies.

So may my love and passion,
That are darkness in the Abyss,
Be, in the heights of being,
All brilliance and bliss.

A LIFE 1957

With kingcups from the meadow
And bluebells from the wood
My boyish heart was mirthful
Before I understood
Aught evil or aught good.

At dawning adolescence,
As dreamer is by drums
I was startled by the odour
That from ancient gardens comes
Of starred chrysanthemums.

In pride of youth, unhindered,
I plucked whatever grows.
If my left hand clasped a lily
My right would fast enclose,
Set round with thorns, a rose.

Magnolia and hibiscus
In manhood showered like rain,
With orchid and datúra –
Flowers dealing bliss and bane
And madness to the brain.

All earthly blossoms scattered,
In middle and old age
With one white unfading lotus
Let me fare from stage to stage
Till ends my pilgrimage.

TRIOLET

A sweet singing bird
In his summer array
This morning I heard
As he perched on the spray,
A sweet singing bird
With his little heart stirred
This fine morning in May —
A sweet singing bird
In his summer array.

QUATRAIN

Peach-bloom, each Springtide, fills my heart with grief
That the so beautiful should be so brief.
This year, more bright than bloom of peach *you* come,
And grief is now so deep that it is dumb.

QUATRAIN

What though so near upon the tree
The golden apples bob and dance?
Around them, like a dragon coiled,
Insuperable circumstance!

STANZAS

If but the soil were richer
'Twould ask no gardener's art:
And lyric flowers would overspread
The greensward of my heart.

The odes would tower like cedars,
Your name bloom like the rose, —
If but the soil were richer
Nor strewn with rocks of prose.

COUPLET

What though the mining's done, th' ore told?
While the vein lasted, it was gold.

SPRING – WINTER

The hills of the horizon
With snow are dappled round.
White blooms the sweet plum-blossom
Six foot above the ground.

As a bird in the blue ether
My joy is on the wing
'Twixt the purity of Winter
And the loveliness of Spring.

STUDY IN BLUE AND WHITE

Though depths of perfect azure
Invest the sun on high,
The hills, with haze and distance,
Show darker than the sky,

Save where, as though disrupting
The blueness of the real,
Shine in their absoluteness
The snows of the Ideal.

LEPCHA SONG

The Teesta in the Summer
From distant mystic lands
Winds like a vein of turquoise
Between her silver sands.

In the Rains, with splintered tree-trunks,
Foam, and forest creatures dead,
She hurtles tiger-tawny
Along her bouldered bed.

In Autumn, calm and queenly,
She descendeth statelily
From her castle in the mountains
To her palace by the sea.

When Winter comes, the garments
Wherein she sweeps arrayed
Flash malachite in sunshine,
Gleam amethyst in shade.

Her silver arms in Spring time
She coils, no cloud above,
Around the smoke-blue mountains
And sings to him I love.

STANZAS

From pavilions of azure
Let us charge when night is done
And fight in golden armour
The battles of the sun.

From sable tents at midnight
Let us sally for a boon
And tilt, all silver-armoured,
In the love-lists of the moon.

QUATRAINS

Spring, in my boyhood it was understood,
Meant crystal streamlets full of bream and perch,
A mist of bluebells in a little wood,
And lambtails shivering on the silver birch.

Now, for my riper years, the meaning's swerved
To mountain rivers green as tourmalines,
And galaxies of waxen orchids curved
Against the ink-blue foliage of the pines.

SAPPHO

Men plucked like flowers which pass,
Old nations reaped like corn,
Great cities scythed like grass –
Oh, not for these I mourn

Any more than for dreams that fade,
But I'm wild with grief to think
What deathless songs were made
Oblivion's meat and drink.

'MY SOUL BETWEEN THE FEELING AND THE THOUGHT...'

My soul between the feeling and the thought,
The known and the experienced, would I hold
Taut, as between the ridges of a lute
A wire of gold,

That when the Buddha-hands shall take me up,
And Wisdom hold, Compassion's plectrum bright
May strike, transcending thought and sense, one note
Of pure delight.

VISITING THE TAJ MAHAL AT THE TIME OF THE SUEZ CANAL CRISIS AND SEEING THE TOMBS OF THE EMPEROR SHAH JAHAN AND MUMTAZ MAHAL

I passed the square and scripted gate
And saw the tombs with fluttering breath;
For all without was life and hate,
And all within was love and death.

THE SANGHA

He wanted that His followers should be flames
And burn up to the Zenith. Now they are
Faint embers underneath a mound of ash,
Afraid of claiming kinship with a star.

THE SCHOLARS

Asked 'What is Buddhism?' off they go,
Consult the dictionaries, row on row,
Sanskrit, Tibetan, Pali – German too,
As though it was the only thing to do,
Until we wish, in all sincerity,
A second Burning of the Books could be.
Have they no other word for sick souls full
Of doubt than 'Read my latest article'?
Off with your shoes! 'Tis holy ground! Depart!
Buddhism's in the life and in the heart.

QUATRAIN

What though with cloud the sky be grey,
The ocean wild and dark?
Tonight sleeps in the moonlit bay
My storm-bewildered bark.

QUATRAIN

Though sinks into the western hills
The sun through orange-amber bars,
In silence deep the moon fulfils
Her destined path among the stars.

TO ——

You remind me of whatever's made of gold —
Burmese pagodas, mediaeval rings,
Dragons that writhe on Anglo-Saxon helms,
And curious tomb-gear of Etruscan kings.

You remind me of whatever's like the sun,
Whatever's strong and shines, that burns and breeds —
Sunflower whose aureole of yellow flames
Hovers about a disc of bright black seeds.

QUATRAIN

Better, O Bull of Memphis, that we should
Have worshipped thee, or bowed to Roman Fate,
Than to that One hung on the Sacred Wood
Whose festering love fills half the world with hate.

EPITAPH ON A 'POEM'

For Poetry, this 'poem' shows,
Your heartstrings are the only stuff;
Only for what's mere verse or prose
Mere grey matter is enough.

STANZAS

Back to where the paths divided,
Shouldering past the empty tomb;
Twenty centuries elided,
Back into the Asian womb;

Back into the ancient darkness
Where the golden figures rise,
Peaceful hands and lips compassionate,
All wisdom in their half-closed eyes!

COUPLET HAIKU

Above black pine-trees, on my homeward way,
An orange moonrise in a sky of grey.

LINES

These gods and goddesses that men have framed,
They help not much, for in the end we come
Back to an empty heart, a brain that aches,
And our two hands before us on our knees.

RETURN JOURNEY

Along the tempting byways
I wandered many a day,
But now my feet turn back into
The right, remembered way.

The bright forbidden thickets
No more my steps entice
Where baleful under blossoms
Lurks armed the cockatrice.

Winds the right path how many
A hot and dusty mile
I know not, only knowing
It never can beguile.

Though dense the frowning forests
That threat on either hand
The Buddha's path will lead me
To the Buddha's shining land.

MEDITATION ON A FLAME

Twisting, writhing, leaping,
Low curtseying, ne'er the same,
Burns in its silver cresset,
Blue-eyed, a tawny flame.

Life from the air receiving,
Light to the world it gives;
No winds its pride extinguish:
Because it yields it lives.

Yet drop by drop, in darkness,
Consumeth that whereon
Its bright fantastic beauty
Must feed, or else begone.

For whether fire or water,
Earth, air, or flower or stone,
The seen lives from the Unseen,
The known on the Unknown.

And man, within whose bosom
Lurks the subtlest flame of all,
Must feed on The Undying
Or flicker, fade and fall –

Must feed on The Undying,
On that which has no name,
But which the Dark Sage calleth
'An Ever-Living Flame'.

IN PRAISE OF WATER

All living things should worship
The element that flows.
Was it not from The Waters
That life, at first, arose?

Sing, then, the holy dewfall,
The blessing from on high,
Which spangles earth's green tresses
With jewels of the sky.

The rains, when frogs in chorus
With croaking fill the night,
And peacocks in kings' gardens
Clap wings in their delight.

Sing, too, in all its splendour
Of sound and surge and foam
The sea which is leviathan's
Inviolable home.

Broad rivers that flow majestic,
Small streams that skip and race,
Record! Like their mother-waters
They seek the lowliest place.

Sing the fairest of all waters –
A mountain pool that lies
Unstirred, at peace reflecting
Calm moon and cloudless skies.

THE YOUNG HILLS

Wonder it is to dwell at last
In hills without a human past,
Where not one building that we see
Before us, has outlived a tree.

In other prospects, hill or plain,
As stone men's histories remain
Centuries on centuries, making fast
Present to immemorial past.

But here, where man has newly made
His home, the human does not shade
Back into rocks and ferns and trees
By imperceptible degrees.

Abrupt transition! Naught between,
The subject meets his savage queen,
And man and Nature strive their best
To conquer, breast to naked breast.

And yet some comfort may be wrung
From this: as hills go, these are young,
Being born, for all their snow,
But fifty million years ago.

THE GUARDIAN WALL

With sweet compassionate faces,
Hands outstretched, humanity's friends,
Up to the golden Zenith
The Hierarchy ascends.

In glory on glory I see Them,
Helpers of all of us;
But the loveliest Bodhisattvas
Are the anonymous.

Lotus-seated, rainbow-circled
In the heaven of the Void,
They rear about the race a Wall
That may not be destroyed.

Its base is built of coral –
The blood that They have shed;
Its turrets sheerest diamond –
The life of purity led.

O Hierarchy Celestial,
O Tara, from Thy throne,
Grant that in Thy Great Guardian Wall
My life may be one stone!

RHYMED HAIKU

Old frog on the brink
Of the lotus pond jumped in –
Not stopping to think.

HAIKU

Visitors all day!
Morning mist, afternoon flowers –
And now the full moon.

QUATRAIN

The periwinkle flowers among the stones;
Where naught else lives, it grows –
A common hardy plant, scarce beautiful,
That shall outlast the rose.

SIDDHARTHA'S DREAM

Mahavastu, Vol.II, pp. 131-2

From the four compass-points a green, a gold,
A red and a blue vulture, birds of prey,
Come swooping down; they kiss Thy sacred feet,
And fly all white away.

Bound by their several duties, warrior, priest,
Trader and serf, for refuge come to Thee,
Follow one Path, and, having followed, all
Become for ever free.

THE THREE MARKS

Impermanent, impermanent!
Whatever flowers must fade.
The world's most white perfection
In dust at last is laid.

Miserable, ah miserable!
Commixed with bale our bliss,
For pleasure's fanged and poisonous
As any viper's kiss.

Substanceless, oh substanceless!
A bubble or a star,
Like waves that dance on water
Nor things nor nothings are.

Wisely thus existence viewing
The Buddha's child shall be
From this world of flame and shadow
Into Boundless Light set free.

THREE COUPLET HAIKUS

I.
How bare and dead the branch! But look, again
Burst forth pink buds, as soon as touched by rain.

II.
The red leaf falls upon the lake below.
Ah well, perhaps the water's lovelier so!

III.
Though vigorously the high wind shakes the bough,
The unripe fruit sticks on to it, somehow.

THE BUDDHA*

Lean, strenuous, resolute, He passed His days
Trudging in dust-stained clouts the forest paths;
Stood as a beggar at the beggar's door
For alms, and more than kingly, spoke with kings.
Only when blue-black elephants of heaven
With bellowings filled the vast plains of the sky
Sat He aloof, and listened, heart at ease,
To the soft thunder of the rain on leaves.
Else was He as the sun unwearying
Full five-and-forty years, and as the sun
Shed upon all the beams of truth and peace.
This did He out of love for all that lives.

They carved Him out of sandal, chipped from stone
The Ever-moving, cast in rigid bronze
Him Who was Life itself, and made Him sit,
Hands idly folded, for a thousand years
Immobile in the incensed image-house;
They gilded Him till He was sick with gold.

And underneath the shadow of the shrine
They sauntered in their yellow silken robes,
Or – lolled replete on purple-cushioned thrones –
In sleepy stanzas droned His vigorous words
To gentle flutterings of jewelled fans…

Arise, O Lord, and with Thy dust-stained feet
Walk not the roads of India but the world!
Shake from the slumber of a thousand years
Thy dream-mazed fold! Burn as a Fire for men!

TIBETAN REFUGEE

You were my mother once, the Scriptures say,
A hundred or ten thousand lives ago,
And now with bloodstained feet you trudge the roads
Of India, exiled from your native land.
Driven, not exiled! The barbarian horde
That burned down temples, looted monasteries,
Tortured to death old holy lamas, they
That stood your husband up against a wall
And shot him, sent your brothers and your sons
To prison for a sullen look or word, –
Even they who on the holy citadel
Set their unholy flag, the flag of blood, –
They drove you forth with terror of the whip
And torment of the unfilled belly. You
Were working on the roads. Twelve hours a day
Breaking the stones, and you were seven months pregnant.
One night you slipped away. A month it took you
To reach the Indian border. On the way
Was born the baby strapped upon your back,
Born by the roadside. But you could not wait,
And feeble as you were pressed on and on
Through leech-infested jungle, dark and rain,
While all the time the dread of what might come
Behind you, drummed like madness in your heart.
Mother, you do not listen to your son!
Your eyes are dull and vacant, you do not hear
Your infant crying for your breast, nor see
Kind faces round you, hands outstretched to aid!
Above the clouds you see, as in a dream,
The golden roofs of the Potála gleam.

POINTS OF VIEW

The politician on the platform
Is sleek, unctuous and smiling.
He is impeccably dressed
In the best silk handloom cloth
And wears a dazzling white Gandhi-cap.
His notes rustle crisply as he tells you
That your standard of living is going higher and higher.
What does it matter, man in the audience,
With the sunburned face and puzzled brow,
That your five hungry children
   Will have no food tonight?
The man behind the microphone
   Is always right.

TO SHRIMATI SOPHIA WADIA IN HONOUR OF HER SIXTIETH BIRTHDAY*

Away with prosy greetings!
Today I cannot choose
But sing in verse the praise of one
Who is herself a Muse.

Full sixty glorious Summers
Have bloomed from sixty Springs
Since for their present mansion
She closed her heavenly wings.

As infant, girl and woman
Into gracious middle age
She has trod with step unfaltering
Truth's arduous pilgrimage.

Nor trod alone; beside her
Urging upward, to the end,
Strode the faithful Elder Brother,
The husband, master, friend.

With him she climbed, and gathered
Rare flowers beside the way –
Blossoms of love and beauty
That fade not night or day.

Though fixed her pilgrim vision
On the summit and the snow
Her mother's heart forgot not
Those who wandered, lost, below.

She lit and high uplifted
For them a ruddy flame
That blazed a path through darkness
And justified her name.

Now as the moon she shineth
In cloudless, starlit skies;
As Sarasvati eloquent
And as Minerva wise.

Or like the sev'n-hued rainbow
That comes to glorious birth
From rain and sunshine – linking
High heaven and lowly earth.

To her all men are brothers,
All guests at Life's great feast;
She's her own United Nations,
A bridge 'twixt West and East.

However much we praise her
Still could we praise her more;
If all our words were diamonds
The gift were still too poor.

Oh sweet the Indian bulbul
That warbles through the night!
But only her own eloquence
Could tell her praise aright.

Hence on this day auspicious
We pray to her threescore
The gods may add – for *our* sakes –
Just forty-eight years more.

SPRING

The quick sap rises in the dry stalk;
On naked boughs the furled green buds appear;
Returning swallows beat about
The clay-built house they left last year.
Earth smiles, and like an almond tree
The Bodhichitta flowers in me.

PLANTING THE BODHI TREE

Triyana Vardhana Vihara, Kalimpong, 18 June 2506

The morning sunshine saturates the heavenly blue as we
Beside our mountain hermitage plant firm the Bodhi Tree.

Oh not with turquoise-hafted trowel, nor yet with spade of gold,
We turn the warm and fragrant mould to plant our Bodhi Tree.

No streams of milk from silver pots, no sprinkled rare perfumes
From musk distilled, or crimson blooms, refresh our Bodhi Tree.

With Faith and Energy for hands, and Mindfulness for spade,
The soil of Meditation's glade we dig deep for our Bodhi Tree.

By day among the forest boughs the peacock preens a listless wing;
No frogs in deep-voiced chorus sing all night unto our Bodhi Tree.

With lightning in its dark blue breast if monsoon cloud appears,
What use? Oh blood and sweat and tears must water well our
    Bodhi Tree!

The heart-shaped leaves will twinkle out, huge boughs bespread,
    and then
May shelter multitudes of men beneath our towering Bodhi Tree.

And so, with joyous-solemn chant, this gold-blue morning, we
Beside our cliff-perched hermitage root fast the Bodhi Tree.

WAITING IN THE CAR

How beautiful is Berkeley Square!
Sunlit in the Spring air
Green leaves float round gnarled boles
Like young thoughts come to aged souls.

How beautiful is London now!
Pink bloom and white bloom along the bough
Sprinkle their odours on the morning airs
Between iron statues in green-swarded squares.

COUPLET HAIKU

Yellow in green, by woods we chance to pass,
The daffodils diversify the grass.

STANZAS*

'Hammer your thoughts into a unity.'
This line once read
The sound came clangingly
Of golden hammers in my head
Beating and beating sheet on sheet
To make the figured foil complete.

Religion, friendship, art
Were hammered there
On the cyclopean anvils of my heart
Into an image bright and fair.
Under the strain the forge-floor split;
Nerveless the arms that fashioned it.

POEMS FOR FOUR FRIENDS*

1. To Ven. Sochu Suzuki
This bright Autumn morning
I have not yet opened my books.
The smoke of the incense stick
Still hangs motionless in the air.

2. To Miss ——
Among the rich Autumn foliage
A delicate touch of green.
In the depths of the misty waters
The red blur of the rising sun.

3. To Stephen
One would be far too many;
Ten is not nearly enough.
When the wind strips the last leaves
Oh the mossiness of the gnarled bough!

4. To Terry
The small blue monkey
Sits on the bough
With no companion
But the bright moon.

TEN VIGNETTES

1.
Last year the lightning
Struck the mountain pine.
This year through the split trunk
Spills the Autumn moon.

2.
On wind-tossed branches
Against blue sky
Chestnut leaves clinging
Like big yellow birds.

3.
Careful! This morning
Down the temple steps
A thick brown carpet
Of sodden leaves.

4.
From the train window –
White gulls on the greensward
Neatly framed
By the white-painted goal-posts.

5.
Lying on the bank
With their hair in the water
How beautiful they are,
The chopped-down willows!

6.
The multitudinous whisper
Of dead leaves
Hurrying along the pavement
To meet the Winter.

7.
White-winged for an instant
Against russet trees,
Flying inland for Winter
Seagulls scream.

8.
To stand naked
In the Winter sunshine
They are not ashamed,
The strong brown trees.

9.
Alone in the fork
Of the frosted oak
The old grey squirrel
Cracks a Winter nut.

10.
From a sky of unclouded
Blue, the sun shines
On flower-beds, statuary
And cigarette-ends.

THE CRYSTAL ROSARY

Tenderly smiling, White Tara
Sits on a mountain of green jade,
Telling through the ages the mantra of Great Compassion
On her crystal rosary of the tears of men.

AFTER MEDITATION

As the last gong-stroke dies away,
Shiver on shiver, into the deep silence,
Opening my eyes, I find myself
In a green-mossed underground cave
Overarching still waters whereon
White lotuses, half open, are peacefully smiling.

CHINESE POEMS

I.
For you in the North, the first Winter snow;
For me in the South, the last Autumn leaves.
Meeting not long ago, we were quickly parted.
Who knows when we shall meet again?
With filigree-work of frost bare branches glitter;
Raindrops on the window-pane make strange patterns.

II.
Taking a sudden turn, the sunlit path
Is lost among the shadows of the dark old trees.
On the black leaves of the coarse wayside bushes
Frost gleams like silver in the faint light.

CHINESE POEMS (CONTINUED) 1968

III.
Façade after façade, along the Embankment,
In serried whiteness Corinthian pillars confront the moon.
Fluttering on tree after tree, beside the black water,
Ghostly leaves, bathed in cold lamplight, shine silver flowers.

IV. *Six Poems Written in Retreat*

1.
Beyond the deserted paddock, a dark wood;
Before our secluded hut, wet strips of green and brown.
Watching the incense burn in this quiet room
We have forgotten the passing of days and hours.

2.
The candle has long since guttered and died,
And in the darkness there is no sound but the slow click of wooden beads.
The Winter moon has long since risen and set
And dawn waits for the sleepy crow of the first cock.

3.
A tangle of knotted branches on either side,
The lichened steps, deep in red leaves, wind to the brow of the hill.
The morning air is tinged with sadness, when we reflect
How short a path leads back into the dust of the world.

4.
A solitary figure, you pick your way
Among orange bracken and silver birches.
What thoughts are yours, I wonder,
Gazing up at the old pine-tree?

5.
Paths left behind, I lose myself
In the violet shadows of deep woods.
Idly gazing up at the old pine-tree,
No thought mars the tranquillity of my mind.

6.
Among dense trees, dimly lit,
Moisture drips from dank branches.
Deep in wet leaves, the muddy lane
Vanishes downhill into the white mist.

v. *Remembering the Retreat*
At the wood's edge, a solitary hut;
Sharing my quiet room, a single friend.
Here on the table, two or three books of verse;
There on the shelf, half a dozen frost-blackened violets.
Hour after hour, we exchange only a few words;
Day after day, I polish a single poem.
Who would have thought it? A whole world of content
Found in these things!

VI.
Heavy-winged, the last crow disappears
Over leafless tree-tops into amber light.
As dusk deepens, the solitary willow
Sees naked branches mirrored in chill water.

'I WANT TO BREAK OUT...'

I want to break out,
Batter down the door,
Go tramping black heather all day
On the windy moor,
And at night, in hayloft, or under hedge, find
A companion suited to my mind.

I want to break through,
Shatter time and space,
Cut up the Void with a knife,
Pitch the stars from their place,
Nor shrink back when, lidded with darkness, the Eye
Of Reality opens and blinds me, blue as the sky.

'FROM THE EVER-FAITHFUL
PRESENT...'

From the ever-faithful Present
Turning wide, we run and play
With the will-o'-the-wisp, Tomorrow,
Or the ghost, Yesterday.

Reft from the living Moment
We dream of 'then' and 'now';
Through 'here' and 'there' we stumble,
Perplexed by 'why' and 'how'.

THE MASK

For seven years a mask I wore,
Secure behind, and firm before;
A mask acceptable and neat,
As folk accustomed are to meet.
It went to school, it went to college,
A mask it was of wit and knowledge;
Older grown, it wined and dined,
Was mask superior, mask refined,
Mask prominent, mask most renowned,
Mask with a hundred masks around.
One day, it felt so hot and tight,
I took it off to say goodnight,
Shake hands, — I think I tried to smile
('Twas only for a little while).
They shrieked aloud with rage and pain
Until I put it on again.

THE MARTYRDOM OF SAINT SEBASTIAN

After Sundry Old Masters

Three nails were enough for your Lord. But you
Hang with your Apollonian trunk and limbs
Stuck with a host of darts. One in your tender side,
One in your smoothly contoured breast, one in your belly,
One in the shoulder, one in the well-curved thigh,
One in the groin, one in the knee, the neck,
All neatly spaced, and at appropriate angles,
While from each deeply-buried shaft the blood
Steals down in thin red unassuming trickles.
Below you, aiming upwards at the tree
Whereon you are bound, the brutal-featured archers
Stand coats girt up, and feathers in their caps,
Giant forearms flexed, and sturdy legs apart.
But you, you do not notice. A faint smile
Curves your calm lips. Your face is half upturned.
Backed with blue sky, you seem to look, to listen,
For that which shall redeem your agony,
O Saint Sebastian of humanity.

ORPHEUS IN THE UNDERWORLD

Suddenly he was there. The darkness glowed
With light, the hollow caves with music rang;
Frantic, to his lyre-music Orpheus sang.
Mortality had plumbed the weary road
Down into Hell, and Pluto's black abode,
Past Charon's creaking boat, past Cerberus' fang,
Down oozing tunnels where the blood-gouts hang,
Past Ixion's wheel, and Sisyphus's load.

Once there, what could he do? He could only sing
Blinded by tears, could only sob aloud
With grief, till after much heart-harrowing
By Pluto's grace he felt, but could not see,
His ravished but restored Eurydice
Floating behind him like a thin white cloud.

ST JEROME IN THE DESERT

Cavern or shed, in the one-candled gloom
We know not; through the black hole of the door
The desert, where red winds howl evermore:
Within, Christ's peace; without, impending doom.
Gigantically crouched in little room,
A lion against his feet upon the floor,
St Jérome sits, the dropping sands before,
The skull beside him where the shadows loom
Blacker and blacker. In a world of sin
The Empire changes hands, the Churches fight
Factious as dogs. By day the old man, stung,
Magnificently answers Augustine,
Then, dredging from the deep, night after night
Translates THE WORD into the vulgar tongue.

FOR THE RECORD

You wrote four letters, one
To your parents, one
To the girl who looked after you, one
To your accountant, and one
To your best friend
Me,
Sealed them neatly.
You wrote out
Two cheques in settlement of small
Debts,
Walked around
Here and there
Came in, went out
Two or three times
Returned my typewriter
(It was early morning,
I was in bed, asleep, did not hear you)
Felt a little uneasy,
Perhaps, for a minute or two
Parked your bus
Down at Kentish Town
In front of an old brick wall
Where it would not be in anybody's way
(After drawing the faded red
Curtains) bought a ticket
To somewhere, anywhere
Rode
Down the escalator
Stood
Heron-hunched in your old black duffle-coat

Hands thrust deep in pockets
Brooding, thinking,
Meditating,
Watched, waited
Anticipated
And when the train came
Heavily lumbering along the platform
Slowly gliding along the smooth shining rails
Suddenly threw yourself under, and in a moment
Found what you had been seeking
All your life.

NEW

I should like to speak
With a new voice, speak
Like Adam in the Garden, speak
Like the Rishis of old, announcing
In strong jubilant voices the Sun
Moon Stars Dawn Winds Fire
Storm and above all the god-given
Intoxicating ecstatic
Soma, speak
Like divine men celebrating
The divine cosmos with divine names.
I should like to speak
With a new voice, telling
The new things that I know, chanting
In incomparable rhythms
New things to new men, singing
The new horizon, the new vision
The new dawn, the new day.
I should like to use
New words, use
Words pristine, primeval, words
Pure and bright as snow-crystals, words
Resonant, expressive, creative,
Such as, breathed to music, built Ilion.
(The old words
Are too tired soiled stale lifeless.)
New words
Come to me from the stars
From your eyes from
Space

New words vibrant, radiant, able to utter
The new me, able
To build for new
Men a new world.

PETALS

Petals
Of the lilac, petals
From mauve and white plumes from
Orchard appleblossom foamy behind
Brick walls from
Gnarled grey branches green lofty
Crowns from
Manycandled chestnut, petals
Of hawthorn plum pear cherry rambling
Rose bushrose bourganvillea elder lime rowan, petals
Dropping on running water, on sunlit silent
Green scum, pink and white
Confetti on gleaming black car-roofs, petals
Borne over ancient chimneys, swept
Down dim avenues, falling
Like rain like seed like swansdown flying
Like spindrift against blue sky like whiteflock
Dawnbirds, petals
Tossed scattered whirling spiralling, littered
Down loamy furrows, sticking
To mudcaked boots, petals
Blowing into eyes hair hands, drifting
Over naked bodies of lovers, collecting
In crimson pools, in purple heaps, pink
Streams along country roads, rivers
Of petals to the horizon, rising
Tide of petals throughout the world flooding
Earth surging into the sky cloudburst

Apocalypse of petals Spring's
Manifesto of petals poet's
Signature of petals red
Petals.

HAIKU

Bank holiday —
Wet sunlit roads reflecting
A million cars.

WISH

I should like to live
In a room with four white walls
Live alone there with one
Flower.
Sunlight streaming in at the window
I would see
Pictures in the grain of my deal table
Hear
Poems in the flow of the traffic outside.

FOURTH METAMORPHOSIS

Too long have I been a camel
Ship of the Desert
Too long knelt to be laden
With other men's merchandise.

Too long have I been a lion
Lord of the Jungle
Too long fought
Paper-and-tinsel dragons

Too long have I been a child
Parent of the Future

Now it is time to be
Myself.

VARIATIONS ON A MERSEY SOUND I

for Adrian Henri

Tonight at noon
The pricetags will be taken off everything
Tonight at noon
Eros in Piccadilly will come to life
Politicians and nuns walk naked in the streets
Neon signs will flash sayings of Zen Masters
And Her Majesty's Stationery Office
Will distribute ten million copies of Shakespeare's Sonnets
Printed in gold ink
On the best handmade paper.

Tonight at noon
Churches will be turned into pubs and art galleries
Stonehenge will be reopened and a red sun
Peer through the stones at whiterobed worshippers
Mistletoe will flourish on every oak
Oakgroves spring in everybody's backyard
Ten thousand Buddhas will hold up a forest of golden flowers
And the Sphinx tell the secret kept for five thousand years

All the radio networks of the world
Will broadcast Bach Beethoven Indian ragas and
Zen meditation music
Science fiction fantasies will all come true
People will break down walls everywhere and plant flowers
Muslim will embrace Jew in the streets of Jerusalem
Protestant and Catholic Irish pelt each other with flowers
All the clocks in the world will stop

Sun revolve round the earth, earth round the moon
Time will flow back to the beginning of things
First light shine on first waters
Agony will be one with ecstasy union with separation
And
You will tell me you love me
Tonight at noon

VARIATION ON A MERSEY SOUND II

for Roger McGough

You are the distance
Between man and Reality
Measured in pilgrim's footsteps

You are the distance
Between peace and war
Measured in broken promises

You are the distance
Between war and peace
Measured in unkept graves

You are the distance
Between life and death
Measured in drops of blood

You are the distance
Between galaxy and galaxy
Measured in blades of grass

You are the distance
Between the seed and the womb
Measured in lightyears

You are the distance
Between the ideal and the real
Measured in wings

You are the distance
Between love and hate
Measured in petty frustrations

You are the distance
Between Spring and Winter
Measured in falling leaves

You are the distance
Between prose and poetry
Measured in madman's laughs

You are the distance
Between last year and this year
Measured in lonely nights

You are the distance
Between Buddha and disciple
Measured in golden flowers

You are the distance
Between light and darkness
Measured in rainbows

You are the distance
Between death and rebirth
Measured in archetypal visions

MOTHER

Three weeks before he died
(That is, before he committed suicide)
Terry
Made a hollow pottery head
Blackbald hideous, huge
Aztec eyes staring
Sanpaku, great
Gaping mouth-hole lined
Sharklike with jagged teeth
Was going to
Paint the inside red
Before he died
(That is, before he committed suicide)
So that the red colour would show through
Eyeholes and mouth-holes
Like blood
He called it
Mother
Could just as well have called it
Woman
Or perhaps
Death

THE TIME HAS COME...

for Lama Trungpa Rimpoche

The time has come
For us to lay aside the masks
Painted hieratic masks
The time has come
For us to hang up the gorgeous costumes in the
    greenroom cupboard
To leave the brilliantly lit stage
The applause
And to go home
Through deserted streets
To a quiet room
Up three flights of stairs
And to someone perhaps
With whom we can be
Ourselves

DREAM

Nightrace of silver-white coach of ghostly
Sledge maybe chariot drawn
By white horses, nightrace
Through whitewinter landscape through frozen-
Fast-world. In the back, behind me, –
Arms slightly spread, rime-bright hair
Stiff on your shoulders, palms
Open, cold blue eyes staring, – you
Silverking deadking driving
Towards Spring towards Winter
Who knows.

LIFE IS KING

Hour after hour, day
After day we try
To grasp the Ungraspable, pinpoint
The Unpredictable. Flowers
Wither when touched, ice
Suddenly cracks beneath our feet. Vainly
We try to track birdflight through the sky trace
Dumb fish through deep water, try
To anticipate the earned smile the soft
Reward, even
Try to grasp our own lives. But Life
Slips through our fingers
Like snow. Life
Cannot belong to us. We
Belong to Life. Life
Is King.

MIRRORS

They are decidedly
Not the best, the Graeco-Roman Buddhas
From Gandhara, from Bactria, from even
Farther north-west, from even closer
To the heart of Central Asia, – not the best
From an artistic point of view.
Cheeks are too softly rounded, lips
Too sweetly smiling, and sometimes
They seem perched rather awkwardly
On their lotus-thrones (preferring
To sit on a chair, or stand),
As though golden-haired Apollo or
Swift-foot Hermes, or whoever else
May have been the shapely white original,
Was not quite accustomed
To his new position. Sometimes
They appear a trifle uncertain, not quite sure
Of their welcome in the world
Either among Hellenized Indians
Or Indianized Greeks. And yet
We should be grateful
To the Graeco-Roman Buddhas, even
Love them, representing
As they do the first
Shadowy reflection
Of the goldgleam of Enlightenment
In the mirrors of western man.

SCAPEGOAT

How did it feel
To be left alone in the desert
Loaded down with the sins
Of a whole people?

How did it feel
To have hanging round your neck
Dragging on your horns clogging
Your steps thousands of
Thefts murders fornications
Perjuries blasphemies –
Sins of a whole people
For a whole year?
How did it feel
To be weighed down by all that,
You just a black goat,
Comparatively small?

Vultures circling
Overhead, did you remember
Hands of the High Priest on your head, flash
Of the jewels on his breastplate, remember
The last shouts dying behind you
As you were left alone in the desert
Crushed beneath the weight of the sins
Of a whole people?

How did it feel?

Not so bad, I think,
As being left alone in the universe
With one's *own* guilt.

Mankind should be grateful
To goats.

AT THE BARBER'S

Talkative one morning, the Cypriot barber
Asked me what I did for a living.
'Write', I replied, not feeling
Particularly communicative. 'You write!
What do you write?' 'I write poetry.'

Ah, delight of the suspended scissors, exhilaration
Of the raised comb! 'You write
Poetry!'
      In depths of the mirror behind him
Athenian walls standing intact,
Long-haired warriors spared for great verses.

IN THE NEW FOREST

Summer 1969

Space, infinite space! Heather
Purple to the horizon, wind
Bending the stiff gorse, rippling
Beds of young fern.... By the roadside
Horses cropping the turf, foals
Straddling ungainly, manes wind-
Tossed across slim brown faces across
Pricked ears scared eyes.
                      Over all
Blue sky blue sky blue sky....

Deep in the woods, lost
Among ancient trees, shining red
In sunlit spaces tall
Foxgloves....
           An oak
Marks the spot where William Rufus fell.

CRIMINALS

'The early Christians
Were criminals,' he said. 'They refused
To offer incense
To the Deified Roman Emperors, refused
To fight, insisted
On loving one another, loving
Everybody, even
The Emperor (but they wouldn't
Offer the incense). They were marked men.
Wanted by the police, watched
In the market-place, hunted in their own
Homes, on public holidays they were
Fished out of catacombs, flung
To the lions, tortured
Crucified. Now we call them
Saints, martyrs, venerate them
In churches, light candles
Before their images, kneel, pray, but then
All right-thinking respectable people
Held up hands in horror
At the name of Christian, then
They were just criminals,' he said
Reflectively,
Pulling on the joint and passing it
To the next man.

SANGHARAKSHITA'S VERSES OF ACKNOWLEDGEMENT

Lines written on receiving from a member of the Western Buddhist Order the gift of his record collection, accompanied by some verses

Though one's food is not perfect
It is enough to maintain health and strength.

Though one's house is not perfect
It is enough to shelter the body.

Though one's job is not perfect
It is enough to make both ends meet.

Though one's wife is not perfect
She is enough to keep the home going.

Though one's children are not perfect
They are enough to continue the family name.

Though one's Morality is not perfect
It is enough to make meditation possible.

Though one's Meditation is not perfect
It is enough to support flashes of insight.

Though one's Insight is not perfect
It is enough to reveal the emptiness of mundane existence.

Though one's Guru is not perfect
He is enough to show one the Right Path.

Though one's fellow-disciples are not perfect
They are enough to give moral support.

Though one's Generosity is not perfect
It is enough to loosen the bonds of attachment.

Though one's Patience is not perfect
It is enough to put up with having to live in the city.

Though one's Vigour is not perfect
It is enough for daily practice.

Though one's Wisdom is not perfect
It is enough not to be fooled by worldly things.

Though one's record-collection is not perfect
It is enough to make an acceptable offering.

Though one's verses are not perfect
They are enough to show one's sincerity.

Though one's letters are not perfect
They are enough for keeping in touch.

Though one's appearances are not perfect
They are enough for friendly recognition.

Though this acknowledgement is not perfect
It is enough to show deep appreciation.

EASTER RETREAT

Páck your suitcase, cátch the train,
Eastertide has come again.
Now at last your way lies clear
From Waterloo to Haslemere.

Praise British Rail! How smoothly slide
The houses by on either side,
Until the train, now fairly gliding,
Runs through the primrose-tufted siding.

Typewriter, textbook, left behind,
To higher things you tune your mind,
Solaced, between the well-kept stations,
With tea and Góvinda's 'Foundations'.

At last! In carriage window framed
You hear the well-loved place proclaimed
In Saxon accent bold and clear
Along the platform, 'Haslemere!'

Free, down elm-shadowed lanes you wend,
Where British blackbirds call 'Attend!'
Making your way, with quiet elation,
To 'Keffolds', brown rice, and meditation.

SEQUENCE IN A STRANGE LAND* 1975

I.
Rusty pine-needles
Sprinkling the green-mossed top
Of an old boulder.

Spring buds,
Half-opened, shiver
In untimely snow.

Two or three buds
Are enough to show that Spring is here.
A few words
Are sufficient to say what the heart means.

I do not care at all
About writing any more poems.
Enough if I can say
How the heart bleeds and bleeds.

White wings flash, then nothing
But blue sky.

A long road,
An empty house,
And at the crossroads
Someone watching,
Someone waiting.

Mandalas
Need
Space.

A gift of violets
For the Buddha
And me!

In the front garden
Red tulips, yellow daffodils,
Stand tiptoe in sunshine
As it falls on the white
Walls where the green blinds
Have not yet been drawn.

Reading
Is not a Muse.

II.
Green pine-trees, and in between
The white box-like shape
Of apartment houses.

The sun sets
Behind dark woods.
Clear voices carry
Over mirror-like water.

Past the eaves of the sauna
Swallows, newly arrived,
Darting, swerving.

Somehow, today
I think of the blue poppy
That grows in the Himalaya.

THE BALLAD OF
JOURNEYMAN DEATH*

'Oh what do you want, you wandering man,
So far out in the wild?'
'I've come to help you build the house
To shelter your wife and child.'

'Oh why do you work so fast and sure,
And why is your line so true?'
'Oh it's many a house I've built before
For many a man like you.'

'Oh will you not stay for a bite to eat,
For the midday sun shines strong.'
'I'll eat my food in my own good time,
And that will not be long.'

'Oh why do you keep your head so low,
And your hat-brim over your face?'
'I would not frighten your wife and child,
For my visage lacketh grace.'

'Oh what will you take now the work is done,
And what is the wage you would borrow?'
'I'll take your wife and I'll take your child,
And I'll take yourself tomorrow.'

'Oh what is your name, you wandering man,
That can build a house in a day,
And will take the living for daily wage?'
'My name is Death, men say.'

FOUR GIFTS

I come to you with four gifts.
The first gift is a lotus-flower.
Do you understand?
My second gift is a golden net.
Can you recognize it?
My third gift is a shepherds' round-dance.
Do your feet know how to dance?
My fourth gift is a garden planted in a wilderness.
Could you work there?
I come to you with four gifts.
Dare you accept them?

HOMAGE TO WILLIAM BLAKE

My Spectre stands there white as snow;
Whate'er I ask, he answers 'No'.
Till I can melt him with my fire
He blocks the path of my desire.

My Emanation, weak and poor,
Lies outstretched upon the floor.
Till I can claim her for my own
Both of us must howl and groan.

Therefore will I, all I can,
Build up complete the Fourfold Man,
Head and heart, and loins fine,
And hands and feet, all made divine.

Banish single vision far!
With double vision ever war!
Fourfold vision night and day
Light and guide you on your way.

In that fourfold vision bright
See the whole world with delight.
Rock and stone, and flower and tree,
And bird and beast, are men like thee.

Men like thee, and women too,
Androgynous, ever-new –
Divine Imaginations free
Exulting in Eternity.

SONG OF THE WINDHORSE

I am the Windhorse!
I am the king of space, the master of infinity,
Traversing the universe
With flashing, fiery hooves!
On my strong back, on a saddle blazing with gems,
I bear through the world
The Three Flaming Jewels.

Once, long ago,
My galloping hooves were upheld
By the delicate hands of gods
As I bore through the night,
From home into homelessness,
A young prince of the Shakya clan.

With elephant, bull, and lion,
I stepped stately round the capital
Of Ashoka's column,
We four beasts bearing between us
The mighty eight-spoked Wheel
That through heaven and earth
Rolls irresistibly.

Nostrils breathing fire, I uphold,
Quadriform, the throne of the Jewel-Born Conqueror in the south.

I am the Windhorse!
White, like a shooting star,
I appear in the midst of the darkness of the world.
Sometimes I trot, sometimes gallop,

Sometimes stand stock-still in the midst of the heavens
So that all can see me in my glory.
My neck, proudly arched, is white as snow,
And my flanks gleam like mother-of-pearl.
Mane and tail are flowing gold,
And my harness of silver studded with turquoise.
My loud neighings, as I paw the clouds,
Echo and re-echo throughout the universe,
Waking those who sleep, putting to flight
The hosts of indolence, apathy, and despair.
Hearing the sound of my voice
Heroes regain their courage, warriors grasp the spears of keen
    thought
Against the day of intellectual battle,
Against the day of the great spiritual war
For Life, Consciousness and Vision, when the bow sings
And arrows of desire are loosed at immortal targets.

I am the Windhorse!
I am thought at its clearest,
Emotion at its noblest,
Energy at its most abundant.
I am Reverence. I am Friendliness. I am Joy.
I only among beasts
Am pure enough, strong enough, swift enough,
To bear on my back the Three Flaming Jewels.
The pride of the lion is not enough.
The strength of the bull is not enough.
The splendour of the peacock is not enough.

With what joy I sweep through the air,
Bearing age after age
My thrice-precious burden!
With what joy, with what ecstasy, I fulfil
The greatest of all destinies!

Plunging or soaring, I leave behind me
A rainbow track.

MAY

'Tis Chaucer's month, the merry month
Of May, when all day long
The earth is full of blossom,
And the sky of skylark-song; —

The Buddha's, when He broke at last
The chain of birth and death,
When the earth was called to witness
And the heavens held their breath.

I.M., J. AND K.

Los and Enitharmon wandered over the graves
Hand in hand, plucking now the nettle now the briar. The sun
Shone on their faces and their limbs were bright with sweat.
'Here let us rest,' said Enitharmon, 'here let us build our bower.
Let us forget the wars of Urthona and the strife of blood,
Forget the flames of inspiration and the terrors of intellect,
Forget Jerusalem, forget Albion and all our brethren, forget
The labours of the furnace and the loom, harp and song.
Let us be all in all to each other, you and I,
Here in a world apart, a Paradise, an Eden, and here
Let us live, drinking each other up, night and day.'

Long Los looked back on the fires of Golgonooza
Flaming against the stars, but at length
Lay down with his head in Enitharmon's lap. She smiled.

Ages passed. The giant forms, covered with snow,
Harden and petrify. The wind howls in the waste.

AUTUMN VIGNETTE

Leafless, the walnut's twisting branches spread
Against the glowing pink of evening skies.
Crossed by unweeded paths, and warm within
Its walls of brick, the kitchen garden lies.

Groundsel and rough grey nettle intermixed,
Cabbages yellow in depleted rows.
Ripening alone in its deserted house,
Through humid glass the red tomato glows.

Deep in the cobwebbed grasses underneath
Their parent boughs, the rancid apples hide.
His arms outflung, above the raspberry canes
The scarecrow leans, head fallen to one side.

THE GODS

One by one the Gods
Of the Underworld emerge
Into the light of day.

Some have raised arms. Some
Bear on their heads
Sun, Moon, horns,
A wide-open lotus flower.

Slowly, gravely, they move,
Emerging from the Underworld
With steady steps,
Walking in procession
Along the curved edge of the world.

Slowly, gravely, they walk,
Descending into the Underworld,
Into the darkness....

And we must follow.

PADMALOKA*

Three Summers and three Autumns have I seen,
And two white Winters, in this quiet spot,
And now the gold shines out among the green,
And reddest roses are remembered not.
For the third time are Winter's icy fingers
Stretched out — and yet the latest sunflower lingers.

Three Summers and three Autumns! In that time
I have made friends with walnut and with oak,
Have clasped the trunks of holly and of lime,
And cómmuned with them, though no words we spoke.
Watching black ants among the roots of grasses
I heard the wind sigh how our pleasure passes.

Russet and gold, the drifts of leaves are deep,
And the third Winter deep will be the snow;
But the trees mourn not, though no sap may leap,
For deeper still the gnarled roots thrust below.
In this quiet spot, girt by the reeds and rushes,
The soul roots deeper, and the spirit hushes.

Summer and Autumn, on the margined pond,
The waterlily's leaves are broad and green,
Soon to be yellowed, with the shrubs beyond,
And underneath a film of ice be seen.
But come first Spring, among her budding daughters
Red blooms the lily on the sunlit waters.

Dreaming and thinking as the Autumn ends,
I like the swallow must prepare for flight,
Must leave deep-rooted here my ancient friends
And go where night is day, and day is night.
Brief though my stay, I shall be thinking ever
Of this quiet spot, beside the sluggish river.

Thinking and dreaming, in this quiet spot,
Summer and Winter, I shall end my days,
Till like the rose I am remembered not,
And life has vanished with the sunset-rays.
Then, among silver lakes and golden mountains,
The new-born lotus smiles beside the crystal fountains.

THE SUNFLOWER'S FAREWELL

Aloft on its tall stalk the sunflower hangs
As though half weary. Harvest long since reaped,
It sees beyond the ivied crumbling wall
Blue-vaulted stubble in faint sunlight steeped.

Aloft on its dry stalk the sunflower hangs
In silence: in the West, the round red sun.
The yellow petals, once its glory, wilt:
Its seed is ready and its work is done.

THE PRIEST'S DREAM

Once more a virgin acolyte he stands
Beside the altar, reverent and demure.
He sees the flutter of white priestly hands:
His head is empty, though his faith is sure.

But now? Awake, slumped in his easy chair
He sees the scattered ash upon his knee,
His greasy cassock – rusty black, threadbare –
And yawns, and wonders if there's fish for tea.

BEFORE DAWN

Cut off from what I really think and feel,
The substance of my life becomes ideal.

A whited sepulchre, a plaster saint,
Is not much use, however bright its paint.

Dreaming, awake, I must do all I can
To join the inward and the outward man.

Death stares me in the face: I watch and pray.
So near the goal, and yet so far away!

LINES WRITTEN FOR THE DEDICATION OF THE SHRINE AND THE OPENING OF THE LONDON BUDDHIST CENTRE

    Flanked by the lotus red
    The Buddha's golden head
And golden body on the altar gleam.
    The white-robed worshippers
    And red-stoled servitors
In through the open doorway joyful stream.
A thousand days of labour done,
Glad faces, as they sit there, catch the evening sun.

    In through the windows wide
    The slanting sunbeams glide,
Setting on each bowed head a crown of flame,
    As from a thousand throats
    Chanted are sweetest notes
Praising the Buddha's, Dharma's, Sangha's name.
The sound of tinkling silver bells
And long-reverberant gongs the mighty chorus swells.

    On this triumphal day
    With gods and men we say:
Long by the Buddha may the lotus red
    Bloom and rebloom! Oh long
    May we uplift our song,
Bringing light to the blind, life to the dead!
From this gold Presence, day and night,
Long may there shine on all, undimmed, the Infinite Light!

TOO LATE

*'The new pope has decided that he will not be
crowned in the traditional manner.'*
NEWS ITEM

Moved by the spirit of the times, the heir
Of Gregory and Innocent puts by
The triple crown, the shoulder-lifted chair
Borne through the crowd, and comes to men more nigh,
Pastoral now and not pontifical
As when he trod the necks of princes all.

But what are these grey shapes that float athwart
The cúrtailed pomp? What makes the taper stir?
From racks in dungeons, stakes in public squares, –
From Béziers, Carcassonne, and Montségur, –
The victims of each cruel pontificate,
Long silenced, cry 'Alas! Too late! Too late!'

THE SIRENS

They sing with fairest looks and sweetest breath,
While all below is darkness, stench, and death.

1979 ALEXANDRINES PERHAPS

'An ineffectual angel', unable to do
Anything very practical, or to follow through
Ideas to the end, —beautiful, soft in the brain, —
'Beating in the void his luminous wings in vain.'

That was Matthew Arnold's well known estimáte
Of Shelley the poet: a pitiful creature, but great.
One would have thought that Matthew, in front of Percy,
Would have fallen on his knees and begged for mercy.

But no, the critic, whether lover or hater,
Invariably trips over the creator.
Creators are stumbling-blocks and stones of offence
To those who are merely pickers up of pence.

Not that Matthew comes in the latter categóry:
He was a poet too —that's another story.
'Mind how you distribute your blessings and curses'
Is the moral of these Alexandrine verses.

(In Racine or Rimbaud, so supple and strong,
Alexandrines elastically bounding along
Are the delight of the French, both the rich and the poor,
But they're not yet acclimatized on England's shore.)

AFTER READING THE VIMALAKIRTI-NIRDESHA

Manjushri sits upon his throne of gold,
And Vimalakirti on his straw mat.
The Bodhisattva has laid aside his flaming sword,
And the Elder has dismissed his attendants and dancing-girls.
So close are their two heads that they almost touch,
But what passes between them no one knows,
Only the golden throne melts, the straw mat disappears,
And the two forms are one, and more than one.

HOPE

By hope inspired, we make – though foiled
Again, and yet again –
A Pure Land out of a suffering world
And Angels out of men.

VERSES

My mind's a silver awning,
My heart a golden throne,
But none to sit beneath it,
Or rule from it alone.

My thought's a pearly chamber,
My love a crystal stair,
But none here to explore it,
Or to climb it there.

My joy's a dome of azure,
My bliss a glassy sea,
But none to make it echo,
Or ride the waves with me.

My life's a rainbow tower,
My death a diamond well,
But none to scale or fathom
In heaven or in hell.

SONNET

Among the mighty mountains sojourning,
Years and decades went by as I beheld
Peak after peak at dawn or evening
Flushed with a golden glory that compelled
An ultimate homage as the day upwelled
Or night descended. Thrones of gods they seemed,
Those dazzling virgin snow-peaks – gods who dreamed
Immortal lives away, by time unknelled.

But now, as in a dream myself, I see
The bare and level fields stretch far away:
Nothing but light and space the scene affords.
Through th' green, a ground of lapis lazuli
Shines deepest blue, and hedges, brown and grey,
Turn to a net of glittering golden cords.

THE SCAPEGOAT

After Holman Hunt

Half hoof-deep in the salt-encrusted sands
Of the Dead Sea, he stops and hesitates
At last, perhaps because he understands –
Far from the rancid herd-loves and herd-hates –
What place it is his red eye contemplates
With head half turned. Beyond the bottle green
Of stagnant waters, mauve-pink hills serene
Border, and yellow sky commensurates.

Baffled but undismayed, his horned head bent,
And threads of tell-tale scarlet on his brow,
He halts before the staring countershape
Of last year's victim, with salt sludge half blent.
Green, mauve-pink, yellow glow intenser now
And throb insistent. *There is no escape.*

RESURRECTION

Osiris is green in colour, dark green.

Long has the embalmed body lain in the tomb,
In the darkness and silence of the stone chamber
Where rows of maidens in black wigs
Walk with lotuses on their heads and lotuses in their cupped hands
For ever and ever round the walls.
Long has the black curled beard pointed at the ceiling, unchanging.
Long have the narrow feet pointed at the ceiling, unmoving.
Long have the fish-eyes stared at the ceiling, unwinking.
Long have the crossed arms grasped flail and sceptre, unyielding.

But now,
Something stirs in the quiet chamber,
Stirs in the darkness.
Shoots, tiny shoots,
Sprout the length of the embalmed body on the painted couch,
Sprouting through the bandages
Like green spears.

Osiris is risen.

HAIKU

Thrown on the white wall
Shadows of flowers
Have nothing to say.

GREENSTONE

High in the mountains, up creeks,
Between slopes densely tree-covered,
In the beds of ancient streams,
Stand the boulders.

Split them open,
And they are pure green —
Spinach green, apple green, and sea green.

The Maoris
Carved neck-amulets
And gleaming translucent fish-hooks
Out of the pure greenstone,
And polished batons
For great personages to hold
On ceremonial occasions.

Tourists
Can buy it made into ashtrays,
Lampstands, and little boxes.

What a pity!

EPIGRAM

What said you, *Short, swift swallow-flights of song?*
Mine like a little sparrow hops along.

LOVELACE REVISITED

My mind to me a kingdom is,
Was the gallant poet's song.
Our minds are democracies,
And that's what's wrong.

Every whim has a vote,
Every passion is free to speak.
Our lives are turned upside down,
With a change of government every week.

Sometimes the 'Prime Minister' pleads,
Sometimes tries to be strong,
But take it either way,
He – or she – doesn't last long.

The monarchical principle
Is badly needed, that's plain,
In the mind at least, if it
Is to be a kingdom again.

SNOW-WHITE REVISITED

Mirror, mirror on the wall,
Who is most beautiful of all?

'*You* are most beautiful,'
The mirror always replies,
Else he'd be smashed into pieces
For telling lies.

So he says his piece,
And stays intact.
We're easily flattered,
That's a fact.

We'd as lief hear the truth
As see a ghost.
Mirrors, mirrors on the wall,
Know this better than most.

Truth can appal.

THE REALMS OF EXISTENCE AS DEPICTED IN THE TIBETAN WHEEL OF LIFE

Six Sonnets

1. THE REALM OF THE GODS
The gods, throned in their radiant overworld,
Are loath to spare a thought for human care,
But drain the blissful nectar unaware
Of human labours to perdition hurled,
And human lives away in shipwreck whirled,
And human hearts abandoned to despair.
Smiling they sit, as ever young and fair,
With fingers round soft fingers tenderly curled.

But hark! the music of impermanence
From the White Buddha's transcendental lute
Swells in their ears. With garlands fading fast,
They wring their hands in hapless impotence.
The time has come for tasting other fruit
In other realms. Their glory ends at last.

2. THE REALM OF THE ASURAS
'The Tree! the Tree! the Wish-fulfilling Tree!
Tear down its branches! Bear its fruit away!
Fight off the gods, or else we'll lose the day!
Discharge your arrows! Bring up th'artillery!'
Thus shout the anti-gods, as desperately
They strive to conquer in the cosmic fray
With visages distorted, minds astray,
Mad for the prize of immortality.

Sudden amid them shines a fiery sword,
Held in the Verdant Buddha's powerful hand.
It blazes in those faces void of ruth,
Blinding their eyes. They fall back overawed.
Nothing the Sword of Wisdom can withstand.
The noblest warfare is to strive for truth.

3. THE REALM OF THE HUNGRY GHOSTS
With barrel-bellies, mouths like needle-eyes,
And necks as thin as neck of mountain crane,
They seek to feed on what becomes their bane.
Food turns to ordure, pus, or blood – or flies
Up in their face as flame that never dies.
They feed upon themselves, – arms, legs, – in vain.
They feed upon each other. Oh the pain,
Ravening on that which never satisfies!

Ah drops of mercy! Drops of rare content!
See, the Red Buddha dawns upon their night,
Sprinkling His Nectar from a golden vase –
The nectarous Message of Enlightenment.
There's no fulfilment in reflected light.
Man's treasure is laid up among the stars.

4. THE REALM OF THE BEINGS IN HELL
Horror and anguish! Madness and despair!
Weltering in floods of fire, or pinioned fast
In ice, they see a leprous sky o'ercast
With gouts of blood, and suffering everywhere.
One torment worst: amidst the stench and glare,
Within the crystal mirror of the past, –
Mirror of Judgement, – they behold, aghast,
How their own deeds of blood have brought them there.

Yet hope still springs, ev'n in the black abyss.
Purging with flame, with water purifying,
The Smoke-Grey Buddha makes the darkness bright,
Shining a silver cloud. He tells them this:
That from hell's depth there runs, the past defying,
A fearful, narrow pathway to the Light.

5. THE REALM OF THE ANIMALS
The lion, the horse, the elephant, the whale;
Bulls under yoke; rooks noisily debating;
Panthers at play, and goldfish coruscating;
Snake swallowing frog; thrush picking off the snail;
Bird, beast and fish, the female and the male, –
In flocks, in herds, in shoals and schools relating, –
Hunters and hunted, – eating, sleeping, mating, –
Something they lack. By wood, hill, stream, and dale,

The Dark Blue Buddha shows an open book,
Jewel-charactered on leaves of burnished gold.
Behold the treasure of communication, –
Treasure of knowledge, – ne'er to be forsook:
Deeds of great heroes, thoughts of sages old,
Bequeathed to man's remotest generation.

6. THE REALM OF MEN
Grasping the plough, with horse or ox they till
The broad black earth, and having tilled they eat
(Man's honest labour makes his bread more sweet);
They ply the oar; they labour at the mill;
They sing, they dance, carousing with a will
Round festal bonfires; they build towns complete
With walls, towers, temples, markets where they meet;
They shrink from pain, they shrink from death, – until,

Rising in beauty, like the Morning Star,
The Saffron Buddha cries, 'Oh have no fear!
Go forth, O mortals! Open is the Door
Of Immortality! Go forth! Here are
The Goal, the Way, the Way-Declarer, – here
Are bowl, robes, ringed staff: you need nothing more.'

AFTER RILKE

The poet is the world's interpreter,
At least to his own self. He recreates
In his own heart the things he contemplates,
And brings them forth transformed from what they were
Into a beauty-truth that cannot err,
That cannot fade or die. Though dull ingrates
May mock, no vile disparagement abates
The benefits the poet's words confer.

A tree is not a tree, unless within
The poet's all-transmuting mind it grows
Refined, reborn, — by his own power redeemed
Into a truer life. The poet's kin
Are Memnon, Orpheus, Merlin. History shows
The best but live what once the poet dreamed.

THE STRICKEN GIANT

After the storm, the day dawns calm and fair,
With soft white cloudlets spread against the blue;
Hedgerows, reviving, sparkle with the dew:
Blown twigs, and pools of water, everywhere;
Fresh beauty crowns the broken branches bare,
And pale gold sunlight slowly filters through
The dripping woods; the elms their strength renew:
All things the general renovation share.

All things but one. Athwart the hoof-churned track,
The giant Form that for a thousand years
Sheltered the herds, in leafy ruin lies –
A tangled mass of branches gone to wrack.
As into their dark pit the daylight peers,
Its uptorn roots point helpless to the skies.

'BLAKE WALKED AMONG THE STONES OF FIRE...'

Blake walked among the stones of fire,
And yet not scorched was he.
He sang a song of sixpence,
And songs of Eternity.

Blake danced upon the moony banks,
Yet did not lay him down.
He trod the stars beneath his feet,
And had the sun for crown.

Blake fought the intellectual fight
With burning bow and spear.
We'll need his likes in Albion
For many, many a year.

Rouse up, young men of Albion,
Blake calls you from the fire,
Gives you his fiery chariot
And arrows of desire.

Go forth, young men of Albion,
To harrow, forge, and plough,
And build *more* than Jerusalem
In Albion — *now*.

THE DREAM   *1982*

My heart was held within an Angel's hands.
He looked at it and said, 'It's brighter now,
But still it needs more cleaning.' Smiling then,
He bent and kissed it with serenest brow.

LINES COMPOSED ON RETREAT DURING A PERIOD OF SILENCE

O Sacred Silence, now at last
We let you softly enter in,
Suspending for your lovely sake
Th'unthinking laugh, the mindless din.

O Queen of Contemplation, deign
Within our walls an hour to dwell,
And let no foolish voice profane
Dare to break your holiest spell.

O Star-bedecked, O Full-moon-crowned,
Shed on our hearts your dew of grace;
Teach us the softness of your touch;
Show us the beauty of your face.

Eternal Finger on the lip
Of Being, make us truly blest.
O give us from the ceaseless noise
Of our own lives a little rest.

EPIGRAM ON MOLLY THE MEDIUM

1983

Her skin is greasy, and her garments stink.
The medium is the message, don't you think?

YEMEN REVISITED

Flying slower, flying faster,
Birds through a ceiling of alabaster,
Gold against an azure sky,
Trace in bright calligraphy
On those rainbow-bordered pages
Lore sublime of ancient sages,
Wisdom-treasures of the heart
Distilled in words by subtlest art;
Words that through the alabaster
Make the listless heart beat faster,
Till like an enchanted thing
Anon it spreads its golden wing
And seeks to join the happy birds
That on the azure trace those words,
Truth to other eyes revealing
From behind that wondrous ceiling.

A WISH

Oh for a Persian garden,
Where perfect roses bloom!
Oh for a white pavilion!
Oh for a blue-tiled room!

Oh for an open window
Through which the birds can fly!
Oh for a young musician!
Oh for a golden sky!

Oh for a turquoise fountain!
Oh for a crystal rill!
And oh for a song in the evening
So sweet that time stands still!

LINES TO JAYAPUSHPA
ON HER RETURN TO MALAYSIA

Dear daughter of a tropic isle,
For twice twelve months your radiant smile
Has blessed our dreary London streets,
Whereon the rain remorseless beats,
And where the sun is rarely seen
Gilding grey roofs and treetops green.
You stayed with us to learn anew
The song that had enraptured you
In your green paradise, but which
Had fallen from its proper pitch,
And having learned, you sang as clear
And sweet as some who'd practised here
For many a month and many a year.
But now that your two years are flown,
When you have won all hearts, and grown
For radiant smiles and sweetest song
One of the dearest of our throng,
You must return to your own groves,
To brighter flowers, and warmer loves,
And sing that song again there which
Is dearest, at its proper pitch.
We will sing here, and singing we
Shall hear far off *your* melody
On moonlit summer nights – you ours
Seated among your tropic flowers.

TUSCANY 1983

Between the tree-clad hills the misty plain,
Beyond the misty plain the sea –
A silver-shining ribbon void of stain;
Above, the sky's immensity
Intensely blue, and at the zenith bluest,
As truth within the faithful heart is truest.

On the hill opposite an ancient town
Dreaming, compáct of houses white,
Red-roofed, green-shuttered, some half tumbling down,
With yellow clock-tower shining bright
In th' evening sun, and telling every hour
How time holds all things mortal in its power.

On *this* hill, deepening silence all the day
Inside the convent's crumbling walls;
Through the gloom slanting, many a golden ray
Lights dusty corridors and falls
On red uneven pavements where, long since,
Shuffled cowled monk, strolled courtier, and strode prince.

Below us, at the bottom of the hill,
Beneath black cypresses the dead
Are quiet in tombs, but we are quieter still
In cloisters long untenantéd,
Learning what to be and not to be
Between the olive harvest and the sea.

ST FRANCIS AND THE BIRDS

St Francis in the Umbrian glades
Preached gospel to the birds;
The feathered songsters flocked around
And listened to his words.

Some on his shoulders and his arms
Alit, some on his head;
Whene'er he paused they chirped their joy
At what St Francis said.

Even the solitary owl
Showed his approval too;
He looked out from his hollow tree
And gave a loud 'Tu Whoo!'

For Francis, with a radiant face,
Declared there to them all
How God loved man, and man must love
All creatures great and small.

But now on Sunday afternoons
(Six hundred years have passed)
Come men with dogs and traps and guns
Those happy birds to blast.

They blast them here, they blast them there,
They blast them all around,
Until spent cartridges in heaps
Bestrow the darkening ground.

The cartridges are green and blue,
And yellow, white and red,
But far more beautiful the birds
That sang, and now are dead.

Oh holy Francis, in the height
Of heaven, where'er your place,
Tell me, does God on Sunday nights
Dare look you in the face?

THREE RUBÁIYÁT

I.

Seek not in gloomy charnel-grounds to see
The scattered remnants of the fair and free.
One crimson fallen petal of the rose
Shall read the lesson of mortality.

II.

Sunk in the stream-bed where the hills begin
The wrinkled boulders are as black as sin.
Strike but one blow, and 'Open Sesame!' –
Chambers of glittering crystal lie within.

III.

In Amitabha's paradise, we're told,
Bloom flowers of jade and crystal flecked with gold.
Could but one petal to the earth descend
To purchase it should all my goods be sold.

LINES COMPOSED ON ACQUIRING 'THE WORKS OF SAMUEL JOHNSON, LL.D.', IN ELEVEN VOLUMES, MDCCLXXXVII

Three years in earth had Johnson slept,
Three years for him his friends had wept,
When from the presses of the town
That saw him risen to renown
And in meridian splendour glowing
(Though fear of death was ever growing),
Eleven volumes issued forth
To vindicate his lasting worth,
His learning, piety, and wit,
And wisdom, for most subjects fit,
By Hawkins' diligence compiled
And bound, and stamped, and gilt, and styled
The Works of Samuel Johnson. Grand
In their integrity they stand,
Thrice worthy of the library shelf
Of any man that loves himself
And letters, and humanity,
Even in nineteen eighty-three.
The first set forth the sage's life,
His outward and his inward strife,
His struggles and his victory –
'Lord, I commend myself to Thee!' –
Over himself. The other ten
Were traced by Johnson's vigorous pen.
(Remembering what the Decad meant
You'll own that ten's no accident.)

Heading them all, three volumes stand,
Lives of the Poets of the land
From Cowley down to studious Gray
And Lyttelton (unread today),
With lives of heroes, scholars' lives,
Where courage dares, and wit contrives.
Decisively he hands them down
The fadeless or the fading crown.
Ramblers and Adventurers follow,
And Idlers too, all far from hollow,
But giving us, in language dense,
Solid truth without pretence
Heightened to rare magnificence
By strong Imagination's aid:
Four volumes to be truly weighed
In none but giant scales – the treasure
Of 'Johnson on Shakespeare' for good measure,
Together with the mighty Plan
Of that on which, a lonely man,
For ten years long he dauntless wrought,
And slowly to completion brought,
Till *Johnson's Dictionary* stood
Foursquare, and trees became a wood.
Next, in one volume marshalled, we
The Statesman and the Traveller see –
And the Apologist of Tea;
The Thinker too, who through a crack
Spied Evil, shuddered, and drew back.
In the last volume of the set
Three well-known characters are met:
The Prince of Abissinia goes
To study men (from boredom's throes

Seeking release), but though long brooded
The *choice of life* is unconcluded;
Tragic Irene meets her fate,
Victim at once of love and hate,
And Theodore his Vision sees.
Thus in their various way do these
Teach us, both whales and little fishes,
The Vanity of Human Wishes.
Now in these dark uncivil days,
Where few indeed can justly praise,
These volumes in my hands I hold,
And though the binding and the gold
Are worn and faded, and the pages
Faintly stained with damp of ages,
In spite of type-face that distresses
The eye with unfamiliar esses,
Still Johnson's spirit shines as bright
As ever when he saw the light –
Indeed, *our* spirit's lack compounding,
Shines brighter for the gloom surrounding.
Therefore, – although we do not need
The remnants of that savage creed
Which clung to him as Nessus' robe
To Hercules, who'd borne the globe
With less unease, by Pallas aided, –
Because our intellect's degraded
To whim and fancy, and because
We need the strength of wholesome laws
To discipline our wayward hearts
In useful science, joyful arts,
These volumes on the noblest shelf

I place, a blessing to myself
And others, praying they may grant
What men today so badly want,
That bracing 'Clear your *mind* of cant.'

THE WONDERING HEART

What can it do, when friends avert
Their eyes, or choose to dwell apart?
What can it do when looks grow cold
That once with love shone bright as gold,
What can it do, the wounded heart?

What can it do, when fairest words
Are changed to foul by devilish art?
What can it do when praises turn
To bitter taunts that scar and burn,
What can it do, the weary heart?

What can it do, when in the midst
Of Truth's own household errors start?
What can it do when from the throne
Of Wisdom folly rules alone,
What can it do, the faithful heart?

What can it do, when all around
The fires of hatred leap and dart?
What can it do when smoke and ash
Await the final thunder-crash,
What can it do, the loving heart?

What can it do, when in the night
A thousand dismal shapes upstart?
What can it do when witches prance
Where shining angel-forms should dance,
What can it do, the wakeful heart?

What can it do, when there are none
To whom it may its griefs impart?
What can it do when on the land
And sea are none that understand,
What can it do, the lonely heart?

What can it do, when oracles
Are dumb, and silence fills the mart?
What can it do when no reply
Comes to it from the earth or sky,
What can it do, the wondering heart?

BHÁJÁ, 1983

Behind, ascending by degrees,
The mountain-barriers stand,
And rocky spurs on either side
Enclose the quiet land,
Where fields on fields, now fawn now dun,
Lie basking in the evening sun.

Here Nature with unsparing hand
Gives man whate'er he needs;
She sends the swift torrential rain
That swells the planted seeds;
She clothes the earth in living green
And scatters sunshine o'er the scene.

But most of all she gives the peace
Within which we can find
The deeper peace she cannot give –
The peace of heart and mind:
The peace that monks in woods and caves
Have found before they fill their graves.

POEMS ON PAINTINGS FROM THE 'GENIUS OF VENICE' EXHIBITION AT THE ROYAL ACADEMY

I. PROLOGUE
With acknowledgements to A.E. Housman

Noblest of schools, the Royal today
Is hung with paintings grave and gay,
And rises mid the streets and mews
Clad in a thousand wondrous hues.

Now, of my threescore years and ten,
Sixty will not come again,
And take from seventy years three-score,
It only leaves me ten years more.

And since for seeing works of grace
Ten years is but a little space,
This morning I must go, it seems,
To see the Royal hung with dreams.

2. TOBIAS AND THE ANGEL
After the painting by Savoldo

He sits at ease upon the rocks,
The Angel with the outspread wings;
Loosely to limbs of noblest mould
His rose and silver vesture clings.

Watchful he sits, right arm half raised
In monitory gesture sweet,
While travel-worn the small grey dog
Sleeps darkling near his naked feet.

Caught by that gesture as he kneels
Tobias turns, as in a dream;
Knowing his destined hour is come
The great fish gapes from out the stream.

3. THE TEMPTATION OF ST ANTHONY
After the painting by Veronese

Again with hideous thud the club descends,
Wielded by naked devil's brawny arm,
As, sprawling on his back, the red-robed saint
Clutches the book that wards off ultimate harm.

Behind his grizzled head, her bosom bare
Save for light gauze, a female devil bland
And beautiful, bright hair in snaky wreaths,
Scratches with coal-black claws his upraised hand.

4. SALOME
After the painting by Titian

I.
With looks demure, and tress that down her cheek
Straggles, enhancing every ripening charm,
She holds the Baptist's head upon a dish
And feels his hair upon her naked arm.

II.
Corpse-grey, a cupid flutters on the arch
That frames blue sky, and clouds touched by the sun.
Half hidden by her daughter's crimson sleeve,
Herodias broods upon the work she's done.

5. THE ADORATION OF THE MAGI
After the painting by Schiavone

Heretics roasted for the love of Christ
Can things inanimate indeed foresee?
Between the Magi and the holy Child
The giant pillar writhes in agony.

Fluttering above, a half-clad angel bears
Both crown and wreath on this tumultuous morn.
Oh turn him back! Oh bid the horsemen go!
Better that Mary's Son had ne'er been born.

6. THE LION OF ST MARK*
After the painting by Carpaccio

Behold the Lion of St Mark!
His steps are on both land and sea;
Proudly he wears his eagle wings,
For power is his, and victory.

Opened before him is the Book
In which are written, black and bold,
Those words which to the Most Serene
Like thunder down the ages rolled.

Beneath his wings the galleons ride;
Before his face rise dome and tower,
Together with that sumptuous pile
In which three architectures flower.

In aureoled glory self-absorbed,
And fangs half-bared, he does not see
The beauty of the humble shrubs
That clothe with life the sandy lea;

He does not see the lowly weeds
That pave the ground, and still will pave,
When all the pomp of Venice lies
Beneath the green and gilded wave.

MINERVA'S REBUKE
TO JEAN COCTEAU

My wisdom cold? It was not cold
When amid flames I sprang to light
From Jove's cleft forehead fully armed,
A maiden goddess stern and bright.

It was not cold that day I strove
With blue-haired Neptune on the lea
For Athens of the Violet Crown,
And won her with my olive tree.

Ulysses, Perseus golden-haired,
And many a brother hero bold
Whom I had tutored in their dreams –
They did not find my wisdom cold.

Sleepless am I, nor do I need
The madness of the Bacchic throng
To trace the steps, or sound the note,
For my majestic dance and song.

Whether beneath the Eye of Day,
Or looked on by the Starry Seven,
Around I lead my votaries on
The everlasting roofs of heaven.

THREE EPITAPHS

1. For a Persistent Debtor

For years I bilked my debts, and bilked with mirth,
But cannot bilk the last sad debt to earth.

2. For a Libertine

I laughed at death with women, wine, and song;
But now death laughs at me, and *he* laughs long.

3. For a Young Child

Short were my steps upon the earth, and few,
And yet they very quickly brought me here.

THE GOLDEN FLOWER

So love grew up between us like a flower,
Though neither made a sign, or breathed a word,
Content to watch it growing hour by hour,
And see its petals by the breezes stirred.

At length it grew to such a breadth and height
It stood there like a mighty forest tree,
With thousand glorious petals golden-bright,
And I could not see you, nor you see me.

And so the flower, for both, is all in all,
Though each is in the flower, the flower in each,
And each in each, for ever, past recall –
A mystery this, beyond the grasp of speech.

THE BALLAD OF
THE RETURN JOURNEY*

I walked across to the lecture hall,
The sun shone bright overhead.
Toby was standing outside the door;
'You're two minutes late,' he said.

Inside, the panelled room was full
Of ladies and gents so refined,
All talking about their previous births
And how it was all in the mind.

They talked so loud, and they talked so long,
That they never even heard
What I'd come five thousand miles to say –
No, not a single word.

For they only wanted to sit and gaze
At my yellow robe so exotic,
And watched the gradual growth of my hair
With a fascination neurotic.

When I spoke of the Way in practical terms
They thought it was frightfully sordid.
Toby put on his little black cap
And everyone applauded.

I.M., TARASHRI

Late in your life you found the Eightfold Way,
And having found it, trod it night and day; –
Trod it with Friends, whose praises you would sing
As loud as any songbird in the Spring.
Now you are gone; but only as a star,
Which, though extinct, sheds radiance from afar
To those who on this dark earth wandering are.

THE PEOPLE OF BETHNAL GREEN   *1989*

The people of Bethnal Green are not beautiful,
Especially when looked at closely.
The women are overweight and loaded down
With shopping baskets and plastic bags.
Moreover they have peroxided hair
And fags dangling from slack, loose lips.
Even the young girls, who *should* be beautiful,
Are puffy and piggy, wear unsuitable clothes,
Walk on black trotters, and munch sweets and pastries
With slow-moving hippopotamus jaws.
The men, who are frequently alcoholic,
Have a wife on one arm and push a perambulator.
But some of the young men, every now and then,
Glance up at the pale blue sky
(Sometimes, of course, it is raining),
As though they had mislaid their destiny.

The people of Bethnal Green are not beautiful,
But some of them *could* be.

THE OAK AND THE IVY

The oak stands in the forest
Among his brother trees.
The weak and harmless ivy
Has crept up to his knees.

The oak stands in the forest
With green and golden crest.
The weak and harmless ivy
Has twined about his breast.

The oak stands in the forest
Upright still, but inly dead.
The weak and harmless ivy
Has covered up his head.

The oak lies in the forest
Dismembered and apart.
The weak and harmless ivy
Has pierced him to the heart.

PARADISE LOST

Living in Paradise
Before the Fall
You'd soon get bored,
And with Eve most of all.

Her silly chatter
Would drive you mad,
Till you felt like doing
Something really bad.

When you had that feeling
The Devil would come along,
Twitching his tail
And singing a merry song.

The Devil and you
Would have long debates
About good and evil, etc.,
And you'd soon be mates.

The Devil and you
Would sit on your bums
Putting Paradise to rights
And you'd soon be chums.

Over pints of the best
You'd natter and natter.
Eve, out in Paradise,
Would simply grow fatter.

BETRAYAL

What agonies await him now,
The scourge, the nails, the thorn-crowned brow;
But none to be compared with this –
That treacherous, seeming-friendly kiss.

'A MAN WAS WALKING BEHIND ME...'

1991

A man was walking behind me
Wrapped in a grey cloak. He was walking
Slowly, but somehow, imperceptibly,
He overtook me
And I saw it was Old Age.
'Hurry up!' he said, looking back at me
With a broad grin,
'Or you'll be late for your own death.'

'THE PAST IS IN THE MIND...'

The past is in the mind,
The future too.
Life is a dream, a cloud,
A drop of dew.

The present is — and isn't;
It comes but to depart.
Only Eternity
Can glut the heart.

THE GREAT THINGS
OF GUHYALOKA

With acknowledgements to Thomas Hardy

Pine-scent is a great thing,
   A great thing to me,
Settling down on needles brown
   By Lion Rock mindfully,
And word and image summoning
   To aid my ecstasy:
O pine-scent is a great thing,
   A great thing to me.

Poetry is a great thing,
   A great thing to me,
With gas lamp lit and sonnets fit
   For night-long rhapsody;
And sleeping till the blackbird
   Trills sweet within the tree:
O poetry is a great thing,
   A great thing to me.

Friendship is, yea, a great thing,
   A great thing to me,
When, having borne a lot forlorn
   In patience, eagerly
A bright form breaks as though a-wing
   From out the greenery:
O friendship is, yes, a great thing,
   A great thing to me.

Will there be always great things,
    Great things to me?...
Will it befall that Voices call,
    'Soul, you are now set free':
What then? Pine-scents, impassioned song,
    Friendship, and its liberty,
Will always have been great things,
    Great things to me.

AN OLD STORY

It was Lilith out of Eden,
Half woman and half snake.
She took his heart from Adam;
Her heart he could not take.

And thus do Lilith's daughters
With the sons of Adam live.
Sweet-smiling and cold-blooded
They take — but never give.

TIME AND ETERNITY

Stand still, O Time, that I may see,
Beyond your flow, Eternity;
Then flow again, that I may bring
Eternity within your ring,
And, bringing it, endow my days
With cause to wonder and to praise.

BIRDS AND THEIR GODS

1. Blackbird
Trill trill trill goes the blackbird
At the cold blue edge of day,
Trill trill trill goes Apollo's bird
From the chimney pot across the way.

Perched above the roof tiles
Old oracles he quotes,
Pouring, in lingering moonlight,
His thoughtful, liquid notes.

Stationed at my window
I hear the darkling bird,
And wish that I could give the world
As divine a word.

2. Sparrow
Cheep cheep cheep goes the sparrow,
Pecking in the dirt for crumbs;
Cheep cheep cheep goes Aphrodité's bird,
Familiar of a thousand slums.

Black-bibbed and tawny-coated
He noisily debates,
As prompt in eaves and gutters
He quick-fire copulates.

No wonder that our forebears,
In palace or in shack,
Deemed sparrow pie a sovereign
Aphrodisiac.

3. Raven
Croak croak croak goes the raven
In London's fatal Tower;
Croak croak croak goes Woden's bird
In his flinty Thames-side bower.

Kings and queens has he witnessed
Coming and going in state;
Once, a princess sitting on a stone in the rain,
Just landed at Traitor's Gate.

The day that sees those grim walls
From his ghastly presence free,
That day brings on the Twilight
Of Britain's monarchy.

4. Peacock
Miao ... miao ... miao ... goes the peacock,
Lifting his golden crest;
Miao ... miao ... miao ... goes Hera's bird,
Ensconced in his low-built nest.

Bronze-winged and sapphire-bodied
He eats, nor eats in vain,
Snakes whose poisons make more brilliant
The colours of his train.

Eyes of mauve and violet,
Ringed with turquoise, purple, green,
On a ground of bronze and copper
That shimmers in between.

5. *Owl*
Tu-whit tu-whoo goes the owl,
Tawny or white or grey;
Tu-whit tu-whoo goes Athené's bird,
That shuns the light of day.

Perched in the breathing darkness
Above his pellet-mound,
Through the moonlit olive gardens
He sends his wavering sound.

Wise, vigilant, and fearsome,
He lives from age to age,
Staring with great round eyes
From Athens' coináge.

6. *Eagle*
Kwark ... kwark ... goes the eagle,
Gazing into the sun;
Kwark ... kwark ... goes Zeus's bird,
His task nearly done.

Ganymede in his talons,
He heads for Olympus' height,
Where the deathless gods have their thrones
In the Titans' despite.

The boy of matchless beauty
Is lost to mortal ken,
Pouring the golden nectar
For the Father of gods and men.

MUCHALINDA

Bowing I stand
As I am in truth,
From snake transformed
To radiant youth.

Sev'n days and nights
My serpent form
Has sheltered him
From the raging storm.

Sev'n days and nights
About his frame
I've clasped my coils
As the buffets came.

Sev'n days and nights
Above his crown
I've spread my hoods
As the rain poured down.

Now the sky is clear,
The sun shines bright,
And the green earth glitters
In morning light.

Reverie ended,
He opens his eyes
And looks at the world
Sans surprise;

Looks at the world
With compassion for
Men locked in inner
And outer war;

Looks at a world
Where his task will be
To speak the word
That sets them free.

So bowing I stand
As I am in truth,
From snake king transformed
To radiant youth.

DIPTYCH

One wears a yellow robe,
Neat and freshly laundered;
One wears *his* black and orange stripes
Who once in jungle maundered.

One shows a bald pate,
Round and razor-levelled;
One shows an Afro style,
Spiky and dishevelled.

One has a gentle look,
Soft and reassuring;
One has a wrathful smile,
Fearsome yet alluring.

One chants the scriptures,
One beats a drum;
To one come the high gods,
To one the *demons* come.

These figures rise before us,
Both ancient and yet new.
So Western Buddhists, make your choice —
Or combine the two.

FOR P—— ON SOLITARY RETREAT

My friend has gone
To the Cymric shore,
Where the waves beat
And the winds roar.

My friend has gone
To a cabin on a green hill,
Where the white clouds drift past
And the peewits are shrill.

My friend has gone
Where, men's madness afar,
One can muse on the sunset
And the evening star.

My friend has gone
Where lonesome nights see
Time intersect
With eternity.

My friend has gone
Where white dawns bring
Dreams and visions
On angel wing.

My friend will come
From the Cymric shore
Refreshed, a flame burning
At the heart's core.

My friend will come
Like the heroes of old,
Victorious brow
Encircled with gold.

THE GODS

Gods in the gallery I behold –
All white, all marble, and all cold.

WORK AND PLAY*

'Work is the companion,'
The Sage of Weimar said;
But play is the lover
With whom we go to bed.

Play is the lover
From whose embrace there springs
A Helen medievalized,
A Euphorion with wings.

CONTRARIES

For you the restless ocean,
For me the rocky isle;
For you the fluid manner,
For me the chiselled style.

For you mercurial passion,
For me crystálline thought;
For you the blithe 'I want to',
For me the grave 'I ought'.

Meeting at the shoreline
Where stone is ground to sand
And foam sucked into shingle
We wander hand in hand.

THE NEOPLATONISTS

Within the shadowy colonnade
The white-haired sages sit or stroll,
Discoursing on the highest good
And on the greatness of the Soul.

Gravely they speak, in accents mild,
With many a solemn pause between,
As if with inward eye they glimpsed
Beyond the seen, the vast Unseen.

The young men, seated on the steps
Below, drink in each quiet word;
They may not always understand,
And yet their hearts are strangely stirred.

About the temple roof there clings
A glory, while above the sun
There spin the holy Archetypes
In cosmic dance around the One.

1993 PEOPLE LIKE THINGS LABELLED

People like things labelled. They want to know
If you are fish, flesh, fowl or good red herring.
In particular they want to know
If you are *bad* red herring. Thus it was
That they asked me if I was monk or layman (meaning
Really if I was chaste or unchaste). I pointed
Skyward, saying, 'The stars belong to the sky, but the names
"Orion", "Andromeda", "Great Bear", *they* belong to the earth.'
They replied, 'You are being evasive. We knew it all along.
You are *bad* red herring.' And they threw me
Back into the sea, where I swam
Happily with other bad red herrings. The loss was theirs.

YESTERDAY'S BLOSSOMS

Sing? This is not the time for singing. This
Is the time for reflection, the time
For seeing yesterday's blossoms
Mirrored in today's black waters.

CRYSTAL BALL

Crystal ball, showing
Not the future but the past, showing
Snow peaks, showing
Blue sky, and in the sky
The smile of the Buddha.

MY LIFE

My life is a dance
In which every movement
Is planned yet
Spontaneous.

THE TEACHER OF GODS AND MEN

Satthadevamanussanam

His dreams were visions. In the night
He saw the lords of love and light,
And did to them, in song and story,
Reveal the Peace beyond the Glory.

His speech was music. All the day
He pointed out the Noble Way
To men who, wandering in the dark,
Had quite forgot their ancient Spark.

FOUR HAIKU

Seen through the fanlight
On my way to the bathroom,
A misty moon.

How many inkstains
On its chipped surface –
My old wooden desk.

What's all this talk
Of the ocean and its waves
As we drink our tea!

Midnight.
When the revellers have passed,
A deeper silence.

TO P—— IN PRAGUE*

Defenestration was the word in Prague
Five hundred years ago or thereabouts –
A throwing of opponents out of windows.
First it was Catholics, then Protestants,
Came sailing through the Gothic émbrasures –
Arms and legs flailing, cloaks blown out behind –
To fall uninjured in the moat below.
More recently they've thrown the Marxists out,
This time not literally but metaphorically
(The Marxists, too, have landed on their feet).
Now *you* are there, there in Bohemian Prague,
Prague of Jan Hus and Good King Wenceslas,
Prague of the Emperors and Alchemists,
Prague of the dreams in stone and dreams in glass.
You see the Castle, see the Golem's haunts,
Stand on Charles Bridge, and watch the Vltava flow.
Perhaps you muse upon that century when
Defenestration was the word in Prague.
Perhaps, from those same Gothic windows gazing,
You tell yourself, there in Bohemian Prague,
'Open the windows of the heart and mind!
Throw out old passions, ancient prejudices!
Empty the Council Chamber of the Soul,
And there install, with all due ceremony,
The Emperor who turns the Wheel of Truth,
The Alchemist who transmutes our lead to gold!'

ZEN

A golden flower held up, an answering smile –
Just that. No explanations! Words defile.

LONDON BRIDGE

London Bridge is falling down,
And falling every arch and tower;
And pointed brick and polished stone
Prove weaker than the tiniest flower —

Prove weaker than the tiniest flower
That through the rubble thrusts its head
When silence settles on the globe
And man with all his dreams is dead.

ON A CERTAIN AUTHOR

Myself into his book I hurled
Like Orpheus visiting the underworld.

REMEMBERING THE POETRY READING

Read aloud,
all poems
are good poems.
Otherwise,
they lie dead on the page,
cold Adams
awaiting the touch
of the Divine
Finger.

'SURELY KING MARK WAS MAD...'

Surely king Mark was mad,
And godly Arthur too,
Sending so graced a knight
On his behalf to woo,

Unless his soul divined
Some deeper, richer plan,
Whereby his future queen
Should have the better man.

Perhaps there *is* a destiny
That shapes our several ends,
Rough hew them how we will – or one
That makes divine amends

For human insufficiency....
And yet our lives we must
Rough hew as best we can or be
Accounted less than dust.

THE POETRY OF FRIENDSHIP*

The poetry of friendship
Is the poetry of tears –
Of the dreams across the distance,
The partings lasting years.

The poetry of friendship
Is the poetry of death,
From Callímachus to Milton
And Shelley's tuneful breath.

The poetry of friendship
Is the poetry of fate.
Friends rarely know how much they love
Until it is too late –

Too late for recognition,
Too late to speak the word
In which the heart discloses
How deeply it is stirred –

Too late for anything, when the Fury
Slits the other's thread in half,
Save to urn the long-cold ashes
And compose an epitaph.

part 2 longer poems

THE AWAKENING OF THE HEART

THE AWAKENING OF THE HEART 1949

As children on a Summer's day
In some bright upland meadow play,
And there with laughter tumble over
On every patch of purple clover,
And pluck in handfuls as they pass
The dewy flowers and fragrant grass,
And chase, with eager shouts and cries,
The lazy, painted butterflies,
Or, resting for a moment, see
The busy lives of ant and bee
With a child's curiosity –
So in my youth did I disport
In that lush wonderland of thought
Which blooms within the guardian walls
Of hushed and silent library halls,
And there from shelf to shelf did range
In eager quest of all of strange
And rich and rare and wonderful,
And terrible and beautiful,
That man, in any age or zone,
Had ever wrought, or felt, or known.

In that sweet meadow bloomed for me
The golden flower of poesy;
The violet of philosophy
That loves to hide itself in leaves,
Though from its breath the air receives
Of wondrous fragrance such a trace
None but would seek its hiding-place
Who'd breathed it in when passing by,
Did gaze on me with starry eye;
The babbling brook of history
Ran through that magic mead for me,
And in its dancing waves I saw,
In broken reflex, peace and war.

The classic lore of Greece and Rome,
Entombed in many a ponderous tome,
With all the wisdom of the East
Which saintly sage or poet-priest
Mused in lone cave or solemn fane,
On frozen peak or burning plain,
And all good, beautiful and true
Runes of the Old World and the New,
Before me like a pageant passed
Of rich cloud, variable and vast,
Which on some splendid Summer eve
Of gold and silver light doth weave
A cloth to deck as though for feast
The purple chambers of the East.

Oh, from the dewy Summer dawns,
Upon the sunlit upland lawns
Of thought which opens prospects wide,
Till breathless Summer eventide
Childlike I ran from flower to flower,
Nor passage felt of any hour,
But deemed the longest Summer day
Too brief for that sweet bookish play.

Though dazzling through the windows fell
The sunshine that I loved so well,
And set the page my hands did hold
Open, ablaze with burning gold,
Its beauty could not coax me from
That universe within a room,
Save with in hand, for quiet rehearse,
Some book of more than golden verse,
Or more than more than golden lines
Where poesy with wisdom twines
In double charm, as if a rose
Should sisterlike with jasmine close
And from a common archway fling
One heavenly scent, all-perfumíng.

Thus oft upon a Summer morn
On our close-cropped suburban lawn
Beneath a plum-tree's shadowing spray
For hours entranced I sat or lay,
On chair or rug, with cushioned head,
And converse held with poets dead;
Till, heat-oppressed, I sank at noon
Into a kind of waking swoon,

Wherein the sense of what I'd read,
And consciousness of heat o'erhead,
And coolness of the leafy shade,
In which, with hot lids closed, I stayed,
And murmurous sounds of bumble-bees,
And leafy whispers of the trees,
And street-sounds, faint at that noon hour,
And scent of many a garden flower,
And all which that rich morn had mused,
Were blended, subtly interfused,
Like dewdrops on a window-pane
When the sun smiles, or drops of rain
Conglobed upon a lily's stem
In one bright orb, and all of them
Blent with my trance, and did express
For one brief hour of timelessness
Its mood of utter blessedness.

    When golden Summer's green leaves burned
To thoughts of Autumn tint I turned;
And when they fluttered to the ground
Plunged into reverie profound,
And asked my books to solve for me
The riddle of mortality.

    How oft before the crackling blaze
Of well-lit fires on Winter days –
Log-fires whereon, at half-past three,
The cheerful kettle sang for tea –
Have I, ensconced in hearth-side seat,
With fireward-stretching legs and feet,

Dreamed all a drear December day
O'er some rare lyric of Cathay,
And felt its subtlety of art
Quicken the blood within my heart!

   A small, quiet chamber of my own,
Where I would read or muse alone,
Had I that youthful study-tide
Upon the house's garden side,
Whence I could watch the Summer dawn
Bedew the bloom-surrounded lawn,
And glimpse the white patch that discloses
My father busy with his roses;
But where, more oft, with loving looks,
I gazed upon my rows of books
(For every one that I could see
To me meant 'Open, Sesame!')
Until not merely days I thought,
But life itself, for learning short,
And yearned, with foolish boyish tears,
To study for a thousand years.

   Thus in the Spring-tide of my days
I trod entranced those meadowy ways
Whose beauty bloomed for such as me
In richly-volumed library,
And flitted there, with eager look,
From shelf to shelf, and book to book,
As in a Summer meadow sweet
A child will flash on dancing feet,
Minute by minute, hour by hour,
With laughter shrill from flower to flower.

What time such youthful bookish sport,
And ardent quest, and burning thought,
Unfroze the fountain of my mind
I lived at home with parents kind,
And with us, like a loved relation,
Stayed leisure, nurse of contemplation;
And in our quiet suburban street
Passed time with dull and languid beat,
And at our table all the while
Did plenty like a mother smile;
And there was love, bright fount of youth,
And in the books about me truth,
Beauty and good — that triple tiar
Ideal humanity doth wear
On forward brow — and musings strange,
And pageants rich of seasons' change,
And dew-pearled dawn and starry night,
And Autumn moons all silver-white,
And many a joy we thought would stay,
And oh, so many a bookish day
My folly dreamed they ne'er would cease,
And, in the world we lived in — peace.

But ah! as that rich month which shows
The gold leaf crops the Summer rose,
And as when cold-month's winds awaken
That leaf itself is twirled and taken,
So did those thousand bookish days,
And all life's quiet domestic ways,

And leisure, smiling plenty too,
And youth, and much of good and true
And beautiful, at one fierce stroke,
With peace itself, dissolve like smoke.

   Tearless I saw, one day of doom,
The bomb-struck rubble of my room,
Whose books, with many a muddy stain,
Exposed to sun and wind and rain,
Rolled, in that war-scarred wilderness,
With shreds of many a silken dress;
And calmly on the brick-strewn lawn,
Which was so trim but yester-morn,
With household things my father gave
Heaped up whatever I could save.

   Thereafter it was mine to roam
Without a friend, without a home,
For many a year, with unquiet breast,
Perplexed between the East and West;
But sometimes, too, the chance was mine,
'Neath desert palm or mountain pine,
In houses, tents and hermitages,
To con the runes of saints and sages,
And thus, for one short hour forget
All worldly fume and mortal fret,
And dream I roamed, exempt from pain,
Those magic meadows once again,
And ranged, as in my happy youth,
Those flowers of beauty, good and truth.

As in some upland meadow play
Those children on a Summer's day,
Without a single thought of rest,
Till shadows, lengthening from the West,
By slow degrees enlarge their bound,
And evening darkens all the ground;
But then, when that bright day is done,
Stand breathless as the setting sun
To fling all fiery-faced doth seem
His blinding horizontal beam,
And do upon the sudden feel
A tiredness o'er their members steal,
That grows with star-rise still more deep,
Till all their being cries for sleep;
And as they leave that meadow sweet
With nodding heads and stumbling feet,
To trudge the long and weary road
Which winds through fields to their abode,
And drop, not caring now for play,
Their withered posies on the way,
And reach at last, as shades grow deep,
Their doorways more than half asleep;
And as, while being washed and fed
By patient hands, and put to bed,
From very tiredness tearful grown
They raise a fretful childish moan,
And feebly to their father cry
For the full moon in the sky,
Whose beams, with soft compassion shed
The casement through, a sheet do spread
Of dazzling silver o'er their bed –
So in youth's golden sunset days

I wearied of those meadowy ways
Which bloom within the guardian walls
Of hushed and silent library halls,
And there from shelf to shelf did range
Less eagerly for aught of strange
And rich and rare and wonderful,
And terrible and beautiful,
That man, in any age or zone,
Had ever wrought, or felt, or known.

   With dubious fragrance bloomed for me
The golden flower of poesy;
The violet of philosophy,
That loves to hide itself in leaves,
Though from its breath the air receives
Of wondrous fragrance such a trace
None but had sought its hiding-place
Who'd breathed it in when passing by,
Did gaze on me with jaundiced eye;
The babbling brook of history
Ran no more through that mead for me,
And in my restless heart I saw
The deeper springs of peace and war.

   Then from my books with long-drawn sigh
Upward I looked with tear-dimmed eye,
And saw how darkly fell on me
The shadow of mortality;
And when at once through heart and head
A kind of aching tiredness spread,

I fancied that upon my breath
Was laid the icy hand of death;
And feeling their diminished glow
Knew that the fires of life burnt low.

   Oh, in those darkening sunset days,
Weary of meadowy youthful ways,
I learned, from tiredness almost dead,
Experience' flint-strewn path to tread,
Which winds through many lives a road
To Peace, the pilgrim's true abode;
And shed along that weary way
The relics of my bookish play,
Until at last with lighter load
And brisker step my path I strode,
And saw that night, much comforted,
The full moon shining overhead.

   Now in less bright and bookish days
I grope through all those devious ways
Which wind, unmapped by mortal art,
Within man's own mysterious heart,
And in the moonlight see unroll
The wondrous landscape of his soul,
Where all degrees of dark and bright
From lowest depth to loftiest height
Like tiers of shifting clouds are ranged,
And by the fitful moonlight changed
From shapes as though of meadows green,
With small brooks babbling in between,
And fields of poppied corn beside
Some quiet bulrushy riverside,

And woodlands where the sweet briar-rose
Above the bluebelled bracken grows,
To shapes as though of chasms deep
Wheredown the torrent waters leap,
And dreary wastes of desert sand
With blinding light on every hand,
And many a heavenward-soaring height
That wears a wreath of stars at night,
And many a fathomless abyss,
And many a plunging precipice
Whereon the eye naught growing sees
But thorns and thunder-blasted trees –
Yea, and to scenes for which our crude
Earth-scenes have no similitude,
Unless it were, at dawn of day,
The sunlit snows of Himalay.

   Not often do I care to see
The meadowy ways of library,
For every bloom, I know not how,
Seems half as fair and fragrant now,
And rarely, rarely, comes to me
The scent of golden poesy
Or love-of-wisdom's purple flower
With sweetness as of that far hour
When on their petals, bright as truth,
There shone the morning sun of youth.

   For in that meadow green I've found,
With pure white lilies bordered round,
A pool as smooth and still as glass,
Through whose clear, tranquil depths there pass

Reflected, all the day, a crowd
Of changeful shapes of Summer cloud;
And on whose moonlit face at night
Doth bloom with petals silver-bright
That deathless flower without a flaw,
The pure white lotus of the Law,
Which wafts, with all its heart unfurled,
Undreamed-of fragrance o'er the world.

Oh, from those moonlit lotus beds
The sweetness of compassion spreads
From heart to heart, and bound to bound,
In peace and purity around;
And borne on many a votive breeze
Across the purple midnight seas
To far-off lands, at dawn distils
Its perfume o'er their streams and hills,
And drops together with the dew
Upon their flowery meadows too,
Till earth receives, in every part,
The sweetness of the lotus-heart,
And vaguely wonders whence is blown
That wondrous fragrance not her own.

Bright shines the silver moonlight cool
Upon that lily-bordered pool,
And bright, supremely bright, unfold
On leaves as though of burnished gold
Those dazzling petals silver-bright
Which breathe their heart abroad tonight;

But brighter, brighter, brighter far,
From heavens sown thick with many a star,
Upon that mystic lotus-bed
The full moon shineth overhead.

   And as when all their meadowy play
At evening melts like mist away,
And they have trod that weary road
Which winds through fields to their abode,
Those tired and fretful children cry
For the full moon in the sky,
So, having seen how black, alas!
Death's shadow lengthened o'er the grass,
And from my Summer meadow fled
Experience' flint-strewn path to tread,
And seen from that white lotus-bloom
The fragrance of compassion fume,
Oh now, of all the flowers of earth
Grown weary, and the coil of birth
And death no more desiring, I
Dissolve in yearning tears and cry
For that full moon whose beams are sent
From wisdom's star-strewn firmament –
The Full Moon of Enlightenment.

   Nor ever shall I cease to cry
And stretch my arms towards the sky
Until that dazzling orb depart
From heaven, to shine within my heart,
And yet, though there its beauty reign,
Still in the heaven of heavens remain.
Then, only then, for me may cease

The well-nigh endless road to peace,
And all things be, life's journey ended,
In all-at-one-ment fused and blended,
And there at last, no more apart,
Awaken to the Buddha-Heart.

THE VEIL OF STARS

THE VEIL OF STARS 1950-1953

I
The coming of love is mysterious as the flight of a bird from unknown lands,
Its going mysterious as the unseen tumult of the wind blowing we know not whither.

II
What is this mystery of love that has opened in my heart like a bud at midnight,
And sends its sweetness crying through the dark like the voice of one mad with desire?

III
Strange it is, strange indeed that, shooting up through the crevices of my heart,
Unfolds itself ever whiter and whiter the pale green lily of love.

IV
If the flower of love blooms not within the garden of my heart
With what shall I come in my hands to worship Thee, O Lord?

V

Bring flowers, bring lights, bring incense!
Oh fools, that do not know the holiness of love!

VI

I do not want to find out that you, my idol, have, like all other idols, feet of clay —
That is why my love has hidden your feet away beneath the heaped-up flowers of its worship.

VII

Not for your beauty alone do I love you, my love, though you are beautiful indeed;
But because, when in this life we met for the first time, a passion re-awakened within me that had slept for a thousand years.

VIII

I know not whether I love you because you are beautiful,
Or whether you seem beautiful because I love you.

IX

Strange is this love of mine, strange but beautiful, like the pale greenness of the Western sky before the coming of a night of a million stars.

X

My love is nothing but the image of your own beauty reflected back to you from the spotless mirror of my heart.

XI

The echo of the song you sing rings still within my heart,
And is woven into the melody of my life like the thread of gold that
   runs through the texture of all my dreams.

XII

The midnight darkness of my heart is full of thoughts of you,
As the grass of the riverside is with glow-worms or the sky with its
   millions of stars.

XIII

Why trouble to keep my love for you secret within my breast,
When it is blazoned across the sky in stars for all to see?

XIV

How can my heart bear to be ever dressing the perennial newness
   of its love in the rags of the same old words soiled and stained
   with a million usings?

XV

Like a melody so faint and delicate that it eludes the listening ear
The rhythm of my love ripples into nuances that slip through the
   fingers of expression.

XVI

I cannot speak my love:
   It is too delicate and fine for the coarse utterance of words.
Instead, let the shy young grass speak to you for me in tiny
   whispers,
Or let the stars at midnight breathe my love into your ear with
   their million silences.

XVII

Does not the moon speak to you in the night of the fullness of my love,
Or the stars unfold before you the unutterable height of its aspiration?

XVIII

The music of the stars is mine, and the melody o' the moon.
Oh do you not hear them singing to you in the silence of the night?

XIX

What matters it to me that a million lovers may sigh over my lines in days to come,
If today you know not that the red rose of love blooms for you among thorns in the garden of my heart!

XX

What use to be decked with the jewels of learning and pride
When at their terrible radiance the beloved cowers down in the dust with fear!

XXI

The earth seeks to prove her love for the sun
With the heavenly rhetoric of flowers.

XXII

When the flower shrank from the sun's love
The sun wished it was a flower.

XXIII

Bitter as death is it to me that you should clasp your hands together
    in reverence before me,
When I am longing for you to take my hands in your own with
    love.

XXIV

The rose-bud which I have kept in a glass of water beside my bed
Will reveal its inmost heart to me if I wait for a few short hours;
But the secret hoard of love's honey stored within your heart
Remains, alas! sealed away from me day after day!

XXV

I thought that I saw the golden fire of love burning within your
    heart,
But when I approached and tried to warm my hands at its flame
I found that it was only the red image of my own love reflected in
    the ice there.

XXVI

Mournfully flutter down from my heart poems for the death of
    love,
Even as the curled crisp petals fall in showers from the rose that is
    dead.

XXVII

One morning I awoke and found love cold within my heart, like a
    fledgeling dead in the nest.

XXVIII

No, my love for you is not dead, but only so tired out with
  continual weeping that it has fallen asleep in the cradle of my
  heart.

XXIX

Sometimes, my love, I forget you for hours together.
But strange! when I think of you again I realize that the thought of
  you had somehow been nestling beside my heart all the time!

XXX

Now it is evening, and the thought of you rises in my heart like the
  full moon in the sky.

XXXI

This is the early evening hour at which daily I wait and listen for
  the music of your coming,
When all the unlovely happenings of the day are touched by your
  presence into perfect beauty like the sudden blooming of a rose,
And when the yearnings unutterable of a million life-times seem to
  find love's highest fulfilment in a few familiar words.

XXXII

I sit in a breathless agony of suspense in your presence,
As though upon a single flicker of your eyelid hung the destiny of a
  world.

XXXIII

Presses upon me heavier and heavier day by day
The unfathomable mystery of existence.

XXXIV

Though the little plant of our love seems not to grow, and though it puts forth not even a single leaf or bud,
Yet I feel that the hidden roots of it are striking ever deeper and deeper into the soft red soil of our hearts.

XXXV

The beauty of your face was the portal through which I passed into the inner chamber of your heart's love.

XXXVI

Like a waterfall your young life leaps joyfully down the precipice of existence in the midst of the rainbow spray of beauty.

XXXVII

You are elusive as a light wind playing among the leaves of Summer,
Or like the playful brightness of water that slips laughing away between the clenched fingers of the hand.

XXXVIII

Though your moods are variable as the play of sunlight on shifting leaves,
Let my love be steadfast as the shining of the sun.

XXXIX

My love, that falls like moonlight upon the shifting leaves of you,
Flashes all the more brightly for your inconstancy.

XL

You can no more confine love within the limits of human hearts
Than you can catch the showering moonlight in cups of gold.

XLI

You are near to me, my love, near indeed.
You are standing close to my side, and I can feel your presence
  even though you are not touching me....
But you are near to me only as the inaccessible stars are near to the
  lonely hills, and stand beside me only as the full moon in the
  midnight sky seems to stand beside a moonlit cloud.

XLII

Sometimes a few light words smilingly spoken
Seem to bring you nearer to me than the beatings of my own heart;
But the next instant, before my heart can respond to the ecstasy of
  your presence,
A word or glance has carried you far away from me
Beyond the millionth star.

XLIII

Mine is not a love that can feed only upon the sweetness of replies,
For it nourishes its delicate life upon the bitterness of your silences
  day after day.

XLIV

Round and round in the ever-recurring starless night of frustration
The black flame of my love pursues your golden youth.

XLV

I hammer with bleeding fists on the cold stone wall of your
  indifference
Seeking in vain to break through into the inner citadel of a smile.

XLVI

Dashing against the black rocks of your indifference again and again,
The raging waves of the ocean of my love are shattered incessantly into a tingling agony of foam.

XLVII

Better bare-faced hatred and scorn
Than indifference hiding itself behind the grinning mask of conventional regard!

XLVIII

Your beauty is like the inaccessible beauty of the stars
Pitilessly smiling down on the tortured questionings of humanity.

XLIX

Your indifference strikes into my heart a deeper deadlier wound
Than the utmost skill of hatred could ever have devised.

L

Let the sharp nails of your cruelty tear and lacerate my heart if you will,
But slay me not, I pray you, with the ice-cold scimitar of your indifference!

LI

The same melody which flooded my heart with joy in the sunrise of union
Now breaks it with the agony of remembrance in the starless night of separation.

LII

My love is bewildered and lost in the wide heaven of your beauty,
Like the ghost of a cloud in the midst of the moonlit sky.

LIII

Fiercely I battled with cruel words against the invincible army of your silence
Until I had won from your eye the victory of a tear.

LIV

I have made a little crevice of pain in your heart
Hoping that a seed of my flowering love may fall and find lodgement therein.

LV

All over the restless ocean of my mind there flashes only the cold green agony of remembrance.

LVI

It grieved me that I did not recognize you when you passed me by in the dark,
For it felt like a warning that I will not be able to recognize you when we meet again in other lives.

LVII

This love of mine will pursue you long after I am dead,
Long after the frailty of your beauty has taken refuge with the dust,
Flowering into the long delayed fulfilment of its longing
From some other green bud on the tree of the multitude of our lives,

Finding you out and choosing you from the whole world again and again,
Even though you hide yourself on the other side of the universe
In the midst of millions of stars.

LVIII

Though unravelled and torn apart by the pitiless hands of Fate,
The threads of our destinies will be woven together again by the fingers of triumphant Love.

LIX

Even to part from you is sweet, if parting be your pleasure.

LX

The pain of your absence teaches me the difference between the clamourous demands of desire and the calm quiet aquiescence of perfect love.

LXI

Love is like ice and trickles away in tiny streamlets between the fingers of the hands that seek to grasp it too tightly.

LXII

It was desire that dashed from my hands the chalice that love raised to my lips.

LXIII

Siddhartha dashed from the hands of Yashodhara the little earthen cup of his love,
Only that as Buddha He might lift to her lips the crystal chalice of His Compassion.

LXIV

Put your foot in the stirrup of Love if you wish to mount the steed of Wisdom.

LXV

He must pass beneath the arch of Pain who desires to enter into the shrine of Love.

He must enter into the shrine of Love who seeks to gaze upon the face of the image of Wisdom.

LXVI

The music of my life will come forth only when upon my heart-strings play the fingers of Love and Pain.

LXVII

Poesy comes to birth from the dark womb of Pain,
Where it was begotten of the fiery seed of Love.

LXVIII

So delicious is the pain of Love that it has persuaded me into the love of Pain.

LXIX

The pain of loving is surpassed only by the pain of not loving.

LXX

It was pain that bore to me in careful hands the bottomless cup of joy.

LXXI

The red wound made by the sunset of love has healed within my heart,
And in the darkness I see that the sky is full of stars.

LXII

There is no wound man can give
That nature cannot heal.

LXXIII

Be like wax beneath the signet of green jade that Nature wears upon her hand,
And she will stamp deep upon your heart the secret emblem of her ineffable peace.

LXXIV

The silence and peace of the old hills sinks ever deeper and deeper into my heart,
Until it seems as though the clouds were resting on my shoulders and my head was crowned with stars.

LXXV

Sitting for hours and hours among the calm, quiet, kind old hills,
I feel that somewhere behind the veil of things there is a Friend;
Walking all day upon the soft green hillside grass,
I feel that I have touched with my lips the finger-tips of Reality.

LXXVI

What is it that these ancient hills are trying to speak out to me from the wordless depth of their silence?

LXXVII
Oh living, breathing Silence,
That integrates with the soundless music of its almighty harmony
   the harsh dissonance of mortal lives!

LXXVIII
Now the sunset glows red in the West, and the mountain with its
   two or three white clouds
Looks like an old man sitting beside the fire with his children in
   their night-gowns on his knee.

LXXIX
Night broods upon the hills like a great bird with downy purple
   wings outstretched
And bearing a crest of dazzling stars.

LXXX
The cherry-blossom shows like a blush on the dark blue cheek of
   the hills.

LXXXI
What is love but the rosy tinge at the edge of the white petal of the
   lotus of Compassion.

LXXXII
Remember that which shines in brightness above your head;
But do not forget that which lies folded in shadows beneath your
   feet.
The stems of the bamboo shoot upward into the sky;
But their leaves, like green fingers, point downward to the earth.

LXXXIII

My love for thee is not alien to the stars,
But whispers in my ear the secrets of the Void.

LXXXIV

Lamp-like, your beauty lights my path through the dark labyrinth of passion into the white simplicity of love.

LXXXXV

Though housed in the shabby scabbard of desire
The blade of love is bright and keen enough to cut asunder the cords of self.

LXXXVI

All the tears of desire reflect only the agony of its own frustration,
But in a single tear-drop of compassion are mirrored all the sorrows and miseries of the world.

LXXXVII

Desire seeks to possess and dominate the lives of others,
Love simply to sacrifice its own.

LXXXVIII

Break up all thy worldly good for fuel,
But keep, at all costs, the flame of love burning day and night in the house of thy life.

LXXXIX

All the riches accumulated by Desire are poverty indeed,
But in the beggary of Love that gives its all is a treasure inexhaustible.

XC

I crave not for the peripheral contact of lips,
But for the central and essential union of our hearts.

XCI

Man seeks to satisfy with a handful of glow-worms
His hunger unappeasable for the stars.

XCII

This love of mine is for you and not for you,
As the moonlight is for the cloud and not for the cloud.

XCIII

When Love has conducted you into the golden presence of his
    master Compassion he bows to the ground before him and
    departs.

XCIV

When the sun of passion has gone down dazzlingly behind the
    Western horizon of my heart,
The moon of love will arise starrily behind the Eastern horizon of
    my soul.

XCV

Time was when, at the sight of you, love ran through my veins like
    fire.
Now, when I behold your face, the moonlight of compassion
    universal floods my heart.

XCVI

What I thought was my love for you is, now I find, in reality
    compassion for all sentient beings.
Thinking to pick up a glow-worm from the grass, lo! I plucked
    down a galaxy of stars from the sky.

XCVII

Seeking for glow-worms in the long green grass of the bank
I have glimpsed the reflection of the stars trembling in the dark
    blue depths of the pool.

XCVIII

At first I thought that my love for you would bind me to the earth,
But now I find that it liberates me into the heaven of the spirit.

XCIX

The Evening Star of love becomes the Morning Star of the life
    spiritual.

C

I cannot believe that the best way of seeing the stars in the sky
    above one's head
Is by crushing the glow-worms in the grass beneath one's feet.

CI

Comes the flower more quickly by tearing up the roots of the plant
    whereon it blooms?
No, nor the pure white light of Compassion by extinguishing the
    flame of the dark red lamp of love.

CII

Love does not argue with Compassion within my heart,
Any more than the Summer flower, if it could speak, would try to refute the ripe red fruit of Autumn.

CIII

Shall I disdain to hold a glow-worm in my hand
Simply because a wreath of stars has been placed upon my head?

CIV

Better a glow-worm if it guides you along the homeward path,
Than a star that leads you astray.

CV

When the horizon is shrouded in darkness I cannot tell where end the glow-worms of earth and where begin the stars of heaven.

CVI

Love is like a pool of water at midnight,
Which shows to us the stars of heaven even though we look for them in the wrong direction.

CVII

Place it in the sunlight of Compassion and the hard green fruit of desire will ripen into the softness and sweetness of golden love.

CVIII

Desire for anyone flowers into love for someone
And at last bears fruit as compassion for everyone.

CIX

The tear of the Bodhisattva's compassion flows through the world as love,
Even as the austere snows of the Himalayas flow in rivers down into the green plains.

CX

It is the smile of the Bodhisattva that flashes upon me from the heart of the golden sunset,
And the flood of his Compassion that inundates my soul with streams of love.

CXI

Joy deepens and deepens within my heart until it opens into an infinite sky of Knowledge ablaze with stars.

CXII

Only fools think that love is something that happens between a man and a woman.
The wise know that it is love that makes the planets join hands together in their dance of joy about the sun.

CXIII

It is this great rhythm of joy that, having given birth to millions of stars in the sky,
Now pours down into my heart and ecstatically begets there the unending mystery of my love.

CXIV

What joy it is to realize that every atom of the universe is reflected in my heart, and that the love of my heart is mirrored in every atom of the universe!

CXV

The sorrows of the earth cast little shadows of darkness across the sunshine of my heart,
Even as the joy of my love is written in stars across the darkness of the sky.

CXVI

Reality is reflected in my heart as love, and this love of mine is in turn mirrored in the all-embracing bosom of Reality,
As though the moon lay reflected in the depths of the ocean, and the ocean in the calm clear heart of the moon.

CXVII

I know that even from the inmost depths of heaven I shall see your face shining out upon me above the utmost beauty of the stars.

CXVIII

The secret of love is love.

CXIX

Let the silence speak.

ON GLASTONBURY TOR

ON GLASTONBURY TOR   1969

Dragons were slain here
Ages ago. Dragons blood
Soaked into the earth, stained
White chalk miles deep.
Now, westward looking at evening, all that we see
Is the dragon's back humped
Half out of the earth (a little path
Running along the spine) and a red sun
Staining the atmosphere, as we stand
On Glastonbury Tor.

   Arriving in the evening from Stonehenge
Long we gazed up at the great mound.
From over the hill's brow the grey tower
Loomed higher and higher as we climbed.

   Michael, Archangel of the Summit, were you defeated
When the elements raged, when the lightning
Struck? Were you unable to defend your own?
Giant spear broken, did you flee
Discomforted, your church in ruins, the tower alone
Erect, funnel now between heaven and earth, linking
What the swing of your sword

Had striven to keep apart, releasing
The old gods beliefs myths rituals
Religions, all that your bright feet
Would have trodden down forever?

    Cauldron unlidded long ago, the Tor
Stills boils over. White mist from wet clay
Ascending, clockwise we climbed
From ledge to ledge, waded
Obliquely through the evening, swam
Through magical shapes, phantoms, mysteries
Thick as weeds in water, through
Voices from the past, visions
Of Arthur Merlin, Cup Lance, till at length
Emerging, the massive bulk of the tower,
Strong, foursquare, stood over us
Threatening protective.
                      Long we gazed
Over miles of green brown patchwork, into
shimmering blue
Distance, gazed
Down into the West, into
Red gold pink grey
Sunset on cloud hill, gazed
From Avalon into the world, saw
In middle distance the dragon's blue
Bulk in fading red
Light, and nearer at hand
On spurs of the Tor,
Black against the last amber
Glow, solitary
Shapes.

Squaring the tower and iron
Railing, and rounding
The railing a human flowergarland, forty
Pairs of hands joined, circling
Gravely on the dark hub of the tower, wheeling
Clockwise in the clear night, turning
In solemn solar dance, in cosmic
Ritual, churning
Energies out of the earth, energies
Out of the Tor, up through
The tower, moving
Silent ecstatic round
And round, slower
And slower, coming
At length to rest, hands
At sides, facing
Inward onto the four walls, breathing
Deeply, breathing
Inaudibly, standing
Immobile now
As the circled stones of Stonehenge.

   Flowercircle suddenly unfolding
Outward, a dark shape
Darts from the door. A voice
Through the strong young body speaks.
Anarakatiya mabana
Katanama ragaliyapava
Hieratic infallible voice, voice
Abysmal, daimoniacal, voice
Of Glastonbury, we do not comprehend
Your meaning, we can only listen

To the flawless metallic sounds
Streaming staccato into the night, shooting up
Through loins lungs breast belly throat, bronze
Hammering bronze, resonant
Bellbody vibrating, saying
Things we cannot understand
In a language we do not know. We can only
Admit incomprehension, confess
Defeat. There is now
No seer, no soothsayer, no reader of dreams, no
Interpreter of oracles to unravel
The dark sounds, to pursue
Through mazes the Merlinvoice, and yet
Now, more than ever before,
We understand or perish, learn
That language or die. Oh but what if
There were nothing to understand, nothing
To learn, what if we had simply
To accept incomprehension, accept defeat, accept
Collapse, disintegration, death, face
Dissolution of the mind, abdication of reason, erasure
Of what can be weighed numbered measured sensed
    known, face
Descent into Hell without hope of resurrection
On the third day. Are we prepared for this?

    Oh I would lie down in the dark, in the depths
Of the sea with my love, I would drift
Red weed in green water, sway
To and fro with the clock of the tides,
Sway as we swayed that night
On the Tor, at the foot of the tower,

In the mauveblue twilight, slowly
Languidly peacefully, forty
Bodies beeclustered together
Heaving, breathing as one.
Oh I would lie down with my love
And be at rest.
                Look look look!
Silently, suddenly appearing
Above the bent backs the bowed
Heads laid together, above the
Greenbrown patchwork humped dragonback red
Light, mysteriously emerging
From among the stars, bigger
Brighter than the stars, hovering
On the horizon, skimming
High above gold clouds black hills, three
Lamps three lights three eyes three
We know not what, one
Larger two smaller, all moving
In fastformation, in orangeoval flight
Triangular, steering toward the Tor
Through the mild blue night, darting
Fishlike to explore, eyeing
Approaching, investigating, visitors
From Mars or Venus perhaps, messengers
From outer space, heralds
Of transcendence, sparks flashing
Between terminals between
Here There, Known Unknown, Tor
Eternity, forces pulsing
Momently on the horizon, brilliant
Terrible a moment, focused

Urgently on the Tor, then
As though satisfied, reassured,
Veering disappearing
In deep blue depths indigo
Distance, leaving us
Dreamily swaying no longer, scattered
Round the tower base, clustered
In groups in halfgroups, talking
In whispers, some drifting
Down the slopes, hailing
With friendly voices vehicles
With dimmed lights parked far
Below.

      Night. Night. Night. Night. Night.
Within the tower within the funnel the grey
Space troglodytes we sat, refugees
From civilization from the world from
Ourselves perhaps, sat
On damp earth amid cold stone. Above
Skypatch glimmering blueluminous. Below
Cavernous gloom flickeringly
Onecandlelit, and in
The candlepatch we sitting
Circlewise against the rock, sitting
Silent at first, separate
At first, but eventually
Thawed relaxed related, sharing
Bread, sharing blankets, sharing
Ourselves...
           On the stroke of two,
Softly at first, then steadily,

Down came the rain, down
Through the dark, dropping
On recumbent bodies outflung
Hands arms, drenching
Hairtangles on improvised pillows, soaking
Icy into sleepingbags cold and clear
Into sleep into dreams soaking
Through manylayered illusion through
Life death space time, washing
Thought washing emotion washing
Perception, rendering
Consciousness diaphanous transparent
To existence to reality strains
Of unearthly music songsound
Approaching receding voices
Vibrations. We looking
Up through the tower see
Starpoints in the skypatch
Glittering intense see
Tower shooting upwards reaching
For infinity, walls
Expanding in all directions, dissolving
Collapsing
As
Swimming in space, spinning
On its own axis, us
And all things within it, cosmic
Dimensionless, the Tor
Soars.

THE CAVES OF BHÁJÁ

THE CAVES OF BHÁJÁ   1985

Often, now, I find myself
Thinking of the Caves of Bhájá,
Thinking of the silent valley
Where they look down on the rice-fields.

Carved out of the living rock-face
In the Western Ghats, I see them,
Steeped in shadow in the morning,
Pierced by sunlight in the evening,
Cell and meeting-hall and stupa,
All so silent and deserted.

Once the yellow-robed and shaven-
Headed monks harmonious dwelt there.
Every day at dawn assembling
In the pillared meeting-hall
They would kneel before the stupa, –
Lofty stupa, hung with garlands, –
They would chant the Buddha's praises,
Chant the praises of the Dhamma,
And the Sangha's, deep-intoning.
Then, as starting with the eastern
Quarter, all the sky above them

Turned one living dome of azure,
And the sun in all his glory
Rose up from behind the mountains,
Some would to the distant village
Trudge for almsfood for the brethren,
Older monks would teach the younger,
And the younger serve the older.
Some again would ply the mallet
And the chisel, cutting deeper,
Deeper in the living rock-face,
Hollowing out another cavern,
Making little doors and windows,
Decorating shaft and lintel,
While their nimbler-fingered brethren
On palm-leaf with iron stylus
Copied ancient manuscripts
Or recorded oral teachings.
Others still, in neighbouring thickets
Spent the hours, so swiftly flying,
Plunged in deepest meditation.
Thus the day passed. Every evening
In the pillared hall assembling
They would kneel before the stupa, –
Lofty stupa, hung with garlands, –
They would chant the Buddha's praises,
And the praises of the Dhamma,
And the Sangha's, deep-intoning,
Till above the Caves of Bhájá
Rose the moon, and with its radiance
Turned the whole façade to silver.

Now the ruined cells are empty,
And the meeting-hall deserted.
Only buzzards can be seen there,
Circling high above the rock-face,
Or else bats, that in the evening
Flicker in and out like shadows.
Not a sound disturbs the silence,
Save when, once or twice a fortnight,
Bands of little, flower-like children
(Streaming from the local railway-
Station just around the ridge-end),
Marshalled by perspiring teachers,
Fill the place with furious babble.

From the steps of Dhammadeepa
We can see the Caves of Bhájá
High up on the rocky spur there,
Facing West across the rice-fields,
Grey in morning, gold in evening.
We can see the children racing
Back and forth along the terrace,
Dots of green and red and yellow;
We can even hear their babble,
Hear it thin and faint with distance
Like the hum of a mosquito.
For, within the silent valley,
With its back against the mountains
We have built a place of refuge.
Dhammadeepa – thus we call it,
'Light of Dhamma,' 'Dhamma-Island.'
On the solid rock we built it,
Built it well with stone and mortar,

Laid the red tiles on the rafters,
Painted it all white and azure.
Then we sunk a well beside it,
Planted trees and shrubs around it,
Laid out gardens, walks, and pathways,
Till our refuge was complete.

Twenty months ago I stayed there,
Stayed a while at Dhammadeepa,
Saw each day the Caves of Bhájá
High up on the rocky spur there,
Saw each day the buzzard circling,
Even heard the children's babble,
Heard it thin and faint with distance
Like the hum of a mosquito.
Then, one afternoon, I issued
Forth into the blazing sunshine,
And, with many friends about me,
Crossed the parched and empty rice-fields,
Climbed the steps cut in the rock-face
Flight by rough-hewn flight, until I
Stood within the Caves of Bhájá,
Stood within the meeting-hall where
Long ago the monks, assembling
In the morning and the evening,
Loud would chant the Buddha's praises,
And the praises of the Dhamma,
And the Sangha's, deep-intoning.

Often, now, I find myself
Thinking of the Caves of Bhájá
Thinking of the quiet valley
Where they look down on the rice-fields.

But it's not of mighty pillars
On their patient heads supporting
Rock-cut vaulting that I'm thinking,
Distant from the Caves of Bhájá,
Nor of that impassive stupa,
Lofty still, unhung with garlands.
No, not even of our refuge,
Dhammadeepa, am I thinking,
Not of the ten days I spent there,
Nor the friends who came to see me,
Nor the meeting that we held there,
When we raised the glorious banner,
Five-hued, of the Buddha's Teaching.
For, when now I find myself
Thinking of the Caves of Bhájá
It is always of our noble-
Hearted Maha Dhammaveera,
Our 'Great Hero of the Dhamma,'
Our old warrior, that I'm thinking.

'When I die,' he said, 'cremate me
Here within this quiet valley.
Build a stupa for my ashes –
No, not in the Caves of Bhájá
But beside our Dhammadeepa.'

Scarce a month ago he came there,
Came to lovely Dhammadeepa,
Came, as ever, friendly, cheerful,
Came, as ever, kindly, helpful,
Came on what – though no one knew it
Save himself – would be his last and
Best retreat at Dhammadeepa.
There, among his friends and brethren,
Day by day he grew more happy, –
Grew more radiant, – even as the
Moon, above the rock-face rising,
Night by night increased in splendour:
Happy kneeling in the shrine-room
Chanting loud the Buddha's praises,
And the praises of the Dhamma,
And the Sangha's, loud and fervent,
While the white wreaths of the incense
Curled above the small red roses,
Curled above the lighted candles;
Happy squatting in the sunshine
With his well-loved Dhamma-cronies;
Happy talking, joking, eating;
Happy washing clothes and dishes;
Happy when the time of silence,
On the whole retreat descending,
Brought refreshment; happy sitting
On his meditation cushion.

Thus it was that when the full-moon
Rose at last above the rock-face
Our Great Hero's heart was filled with
Happiness as she with splendour.

Long he sat there in the shrine-room,
Long he meditated; wrote a
Note and pinned it to his pillow:
'My own action this: none other's';
Then upon the gravelled terrace
Took a turn or two (I see him
Solitary in the moonlight!);
Took a turn or two, considering,
Making firm his resolution,
Weighing all things in the balance;
Saw the scale of life plunge downward
And the scale of death fly upward.
Yes, the time had come now: midnight.
Down he sat there in the moonlight,
Sat not far from Dhammadeepa;
Wringing wet his yellow robes were,
Wringing wet, but not with water;
Down he sat, serene and mindful;
Gazed across the quiet valley
Up to where the Caves of Bhájá
Shone like silver in the moonlight,
Gazed a while, his last look taking.
Seventy years and more he'd laboured,
Laboured for the good of others,
First as son and elder brother,
Then as husband and as father,
Finally as homeless-wandering
Dhamma-farer, ever cheerful,
Ever friendly, ever active.
Much he loved his Dhamma-brothers,
Much he loved to serve and help them,
But alas! his strength was waning

And the time was fast approaching
When he could no longer render
Joyful service to the Order
But himself have need of service.
'Better far this frame should perish
Than that I should be a burden
To my noble Dhamma-brothers.
Enough have they to do without me.'
Strong in this belief he'd come there,
Come to lovely Dhammadeepa
For his last and best retreat there.
Strong in this belief, and happy,
Quiet he sat now in the moonlight,
Sat not far from Dhammadeepa;
Smiled, and then, his robes igniting,
In a sudden blaze of splendour
Passed in glory from the world.

That is why I find myself
Thinking of the Caves of Bhájá
Thinking of the quiet valley
Where they look down on the rice-fields.

HERCULES AND THE BIRDS

HERCULES AND THE BIRDS   *1985*

I.
Pink and white upon the hillside
Down in Naples, stands the massive
Archaeological Museum.
Palm trees stand before its portals, –
Date palms, crowned with feathery branches, –
While all round it, never ceasing,
Roars and howls and shrieks the traffic.
Silent in the lofty galleries
Stand or sit the white Immortals,
With the Heroes and the Roman
Emperors, naked or be-toga'd –
Stand or sit in bronze and marble,
Sad remains of ancient greatness.
Some, alas, are headless, armless,
Some, alas, are cracked and broken,
Or disfigured by the vandal.
There, majestic, stands Athené,
But her hand is Victory-less;
There the wise and bright Apollo,
But his bow and lyre are broken
(Headless, buxom Aphrodité
Shameless shows a shapely bottom).

Yet, within those lofty galleries,
One, at least, stands whole and perfect,
Clean as from the sculptor's chisel;
One, at least, shows undiminished
All the living faith of Hellas.
He, the greatest of the Heroes,
He, the Herculés Farnesé,
By the undelved earth protected
Centuries long, and resurrected
To the wondering gaze of mortals
At the height of the Renáissance
Stands there, looking down gigantic
On this modern world of pygmies.

II.

Later, back at Il Convento,
At my desk before the window,
Taking up the picture postcard
That I bought in the Museum,
Long I gaze at the completeness
Of the Herculés Farnesé.
Brawny thighs and massive torso,
Shoulders broader than a barn-door,
Small head, curly-haired, based solid
On a bull-like neck half hidden
By a beard that falls luxuriant
To a chest of amplest measure –
Thus I see him. He is leaning
On a club of knotted olive,
That head downwards he is resting
On a round and rugged boulder.
On the club is draped a lion-skin, –

Lion-skin many-folded, ample, –
While beneath the Hero's dangled
Left arm, with its hand half-curving,
Hangs the lion-head, jaws disparted.
Stern but gentle he is leaning
On his club of knotted olive,
Thoughtfully his brow inclining,
Resting from his mighty labours.
Simple and sublime he stands there,
Less than god, but more than mortal.
He has slain the lion Neméan,
Wears its pelt now for a garment.
He has slain the marsh-born Hydra,
Crushing with his club the monster's
Multiplying heads, and dipped his
Arrows in the poisonous blood-gouts.
He has caught alive the magic
Brazen-hoofed and golden-antlered
Cerynthéian Hind, the fleet one:
Over hill and dale he chased her
One whole year; then caught and bound her.
He has caught alive the monstrous
Erymánthian Boar, the fierce one;
Chained him, foaming, in a snow-drift.
He has cleansed the Áugean Stables,
Where three thousand head of cattle
Thirty years and more had sheltered;
Cleansed them in a day, diverting
Through their doors a mighty river.
He has chased away the Harpies,
Foul defilers of the banquet;
Chased away the noisome Bird-things,

Woman-headed, with his arrows.
He has caught alive the Cretan
Bull, the fiery-breathed, the white one;
Caught the Minotaur's begetter.
He has from the Thracian uplands
Stolen Diomedés' Horses;
Horses that their cruel master
Fed on human flesh each morning.
He has reft the Golden Girdle
From the breasts of Hippolyté,
But, alas! has slain the maiden
In her Amazonian fierceness.
He has sailed towards the sunset,
To an island in the Ocean
Where the Sphinx's monstrous father
And the progeny of Arés
Guard the Oxen of Gerýon:
With his club he overcame them
And possessed him of the cattle.
He has brought the Golden Apples
From the ever-blooming Garden, –
Golden apples, dragon-warded, –
While the white-robed maidens, singing,
Circled round the sacred branches.
He has into Hell descended,
Dragged the triple-headed Guardian
Of the Gates of Hell, protesting,
Up into the light of Heaven.
Many other mighty labours
He, unceasing, has accomplished;
Labours for the good of others
And himself to purify

From pollution of kin-murder:
(Driven mad by jealous Hera,
Queen of Heaven, he, unwitting,
Took the lives of sons and nephews).
All the monstrous births of Nature,
Misbegotten, slime-engendered,
He has wholly extirpated;
All their foully-nurtured children
He has either slain or shackled.
Tyrants from their thrones deposing,
Succouring the weak and helpless,
Law and justice like twin pillars
He has planted in the kingdoms.
Now, deep-brooding, he is resting,
Resting from his mighty labours –
He, the greatest of the Heroes,
He, the Herculés Farnesé.
There, within those lofty galleries,
Leaning on his club of knotted
Olive draped with pelt Neméan,
He is standing, whole and perfect.
Laying down the picture postcard
That I bought in the Museum
Long I dream of his completeness.

III.
Sudden, from beneath my window,
Comes a sound of shouting, barking.
Looking out, I see below me
Men and dogs from Fiats tumbling.
All the men are armed with rifles,
All are dressed in olive denim;

All upon their heads are wearing
Shooting-caps with little feathers,
While from bulging jacket pockets
Necks of bottles are protruding.
On the slope they stand consulting,
Loading rifles, slamming car doors,
Then with dogs behind them frisking
Scatter out across the hillside
As, above the dying hubbub,
From the church across the valley
Clangs the Sunday early Mass bell.
Soon, from deep within the foothills, –
Tuscan foothills, forest-mantled, –
We can hear the crack of rifles,
As the modern race of heroes
There pursue their weekend labours.
Later, on our walks we meet them
Skulking in the rock-strewn by-paths,
Crouching underneath the bushes,
With their rifles at the ready
And their fingers on the trigger.
Some are camouflaged with branches,
Some have decoy-birds in cages;
Others, from their hide-outs, blow on
Decoy-whistles, sweetly warbling
(Every now and then a bottle
Raising to their lips and swigging).
Year by year they come, remorseless,
In the pleasant Tuscan Autumn,
When the olive-fruits are gleaming
Black among the grey-green foliage,
And, beside the stony pathway,

Cyclamens, the pink and frail ones,
Push up through the rotting leafmould
And the withered leaves and grasses.
They have slain the chirping sparrows,
Slain the linnet and the whitethroat,
Slain the robin and the wagtail,
Slain the magpie and the pigeon,
Slain them in their tens of thousands,
Till within those ancient foothills, –
Tuscan foothills, forest-mantled,
Ever green, and aromatic, –
Rarely now are heard the songbirds
Fluting from the leafy branches;
Rarely, rarely, do we see them
Flitting to and fro like shadows
On the outskirts of the forest.
Yet, though year by year the hunters
Farther have to range and wider
(As the birds, their numbers dwindling,
Deeper shrink within the coverts),
Still, on pale blue Autumn mornings,
Off they go with dogs and rifles;
Still, on deep blue Autumn evenings,
Back they come with bulging game bags:
While, throughout the gold-blue Autumn
Day, from deep within the foothills,
Comes the hateful crack of rifles
As the modern race of heroes
Go about their weekend labours.

IV.

Last night in a dream I saw him,
He, the greatest of the Heroes,
He, the Herculés Farnesé,
Less than god, but more than mortal.
Like a solitary mountain
That, upon the far horizon,
In some long untrodden region
Looms above a barren landscape; —
Like a thundercloud that, swollen,
Rolls up from the heaving ocean
And, above the earth impending,
Threatens to discharge its burden; —
Like the smoke of a volcano,
That, in mighty volumes towering,
Spreads across the face of heaven,
While, within the parent crater,
Bubbles up the yellow lava; —
Like a forest fire that, raging,
Roars and crackles through the woodland,
Licking up the trees and bushes
With its tongues of gold and scarlet —
Thus I saw him. From his shoulders
Hung the skin of lion Neméan, —
Lion-skin many-folded, ample, —
With the mighty forepaws, knotted,
Crossed upon his naked bosom,
While above his head the massive
Lion-head, like a crested helmet
Resting, reared itself, triumphant.
Whirling high his club of knotted
Olive, that athwart the landscape

Cast a black and dreadful shadow,
He with giant step was striding
Ridge to ridge across the foothills.
As he went, he drove before him
All the men with dogs and rifles,
All the modern race of heroes:
Like a flock of sheep he drove them.
With his foot the weapons crushing,
With his hand the decoys freeing,
On he strode – the birds around him
Fluttering cloudlike, loudly singing.
Birds upon his head and shoulders,
Birds upon his beard and lion-skin;
Birds upon his club of knotted
Olive perching in their thousands –
On I saw him moving: – saw him
Pass from land to land, redressing
All the wrongs that on the weaker
By the stronger are inflicted,
And, within the souls of millions,
Sow the dragon seed of vengeance;
Saw him drive before him, headlong,
All the brood of fraud and rapine,
All the hosts of lust and violence,
All the forces of destruction;
Saw him crush the robot armies;
Saw him smash the hideous weapons;
Saw him from their sunless prisons
Free the victims of oppression;
Saw him cleanse the earth and ocean;
Saw him build anew the cities;
Saw him forge between the nations

Golden links of truth and friendship,
Ever-during. — *Thus* I saw him
Last night in my dream or vision,
He, the greatest of the Heroes,
He, the Herculés Farnesé,
Bent on ever-nobler labours
For the good of others; — saw him —
Sun of Justice — in the heavens
Blazing; saw him golden, glorious,
Showering beams of blessing; — saw him
Show how strength, by love directed,
Shapes anew this world of mortals,
And, upon a nobler pattern,
Rears our heavenly-earthly city;
Till, from mortal to Immortal
Changing, after many labours
We, like him, to high Olympus
Raised, from Hebé's rosy fingers
Receive at last the cup ambrosial.

part 3 translations

TRANSLATIONS FROM THE PALI

AUSPICIOUS SIGNS   *1949*

Mangala Sutta

For welfare wishing, many gods and men
Have pondered on 'the most auspicious sign':
Tell us the most auspicious sign of all.

Not to serve fools but men of wisdom deep,
And to give worship to the worshipful –
This is the most auspicious sign of all.

Life in a suitable locality,
With deeds of merit done in former times,
And aspiration to the Perfect State –
This is the most auspicious sign of all.

Much knowledge, and much skill in arts and crafts,
A well-learnt discipline, and pleasant speech –
This is the most auspicious sign of all.

The maintenance of parents past their youth,
The loving nurture of one's child and wife,
And following a peaceful livelihood –
This is the most auspicious sign of all.

To give in charity, live righteously,
To help one's kindred in the time of need,
And to do spotless deeds that bring no blame –
This is the most auspicious sign of all.

To cease and utterly abstain from sin,
Shunning all wit-destroying drinks and drugs,
And to be vigilant in doing good –
This is the most auspicious sign of all.

Reverent demeanour, humbleheartedness,
Contentment sweet and lowly gratitude,
And hearkening to the Law at proper times –
This is the most auspicious sign of all.

Patience in provocation, pleasant speech,
The sight of those who lead the holy life,
And talk about the Truth in season meet –
This is the most auspicious sign of all.

Asceticism and the life sublime,
The vision splendid of the Noble Truths,
The seeing of Nibbana face to face –
This is the most auspicious sign of all.

He whose firm mind, untroubled by the touch
Of all terrestrial happenings whatso'er,
Is void of sorrow, stainless, and secure –
This is the most auspicious sign of all.

Those who accomplish such good things as these
In every place unconquered do abide,
Moving in perfect safety where they will –
Theirs are the most auspicious signs of all.

LOVING KINDNESS 1949

Karaniyametta Sutta

This must be done by one who kens his good,
Who grasps the meaning of 'The Place of Peace'.
Able and upright, yea, and truly straight,
Soft-spoken and mild-mannered, must he be,
And void of all the vain conceit of self.
He should be well content, soon satisfied,
With wants but few, of frugal appetites,
With faculties of sense restrained and stilled,
Discreet in all his ways, not insolent,
Nor greedy after gifts; nor should he do
Any ignoble act which other men,
Wiser, beholding might rebuke him for.

Now, may all living things, or weak or strong,
Omitting none, tall, middle-sized, or short,
Subtle or gross of form, seen or unseen,
Those dwelling near or dwelling far away,
Born or unborn – may every living thing
Abound in bliss. Let none deceive or think
Scorn of another, in whatever way.
But as a mother watches o'er her child,
Her only child, so long as she doth breathe,
So let him practise unto all that live
An all-embracing mind. And let a man
Practise unbounded love for all the world,
Above, below, across, in every way,
Love unobstructed, void of enmity.
Standing or moving, sitting, lying down,

In whatsoever way that man may be,
Provided he be slothless, let him found
Firmly this mindfulness of boundless love.
For this is what men call 'The State Sublime'.
So shall a man, by leaving far behind
All wrongful views, by walking righteously,
Attain to gnostic vision and crush out
All lust for sensual pleasures. Such in truth
Shall come to birth no more in any womb.

JEWELS   1949

Ratana Sutta

Whatever beings are assembled here,
Creatures of earth or spirits of the sky,
May they be happy-minded, every one,
And pay good heed to what is said to them.

Hence, all ye spirits, hear attentively.
Look lovingly upon the race of men,
And, since they bring thee offerings day and night,
Keep watch and ward about them heedfully.

The riches of this world and of the next,
And all the precious things the heav'ns may hold,
None can compare with the Tathágata.
Yea, in the Buddha shines this glorious gem:
By virtue of this truth, may bliss abound!

The waning out of lust, that wondrous state
Of deathlessness the Shakyan Sage attained
Through calm and concentration of the mind –
Nothing at all with that state can compare.
Yea, in the Teaching shines this glorious gem:
By virtue of this truth, may bliss abound!

That flawless meditation praised by Him
Who is the Wisest of the wise, which brings
Instant reward to him who practises —
Naught with that meditation can compare.
Yea, in the Teaching shines this glorious gem:
By virtue of this truth, may bliss abound!

Those persons eight whom all the sages praise
Make up four pairs. Worthy of offerings
Are they, the followers of the Happy One,
And offerings made them bear abundant fruit.
Yea, in the Order shines this glorious gem:
By virtue of this truth, may bliss abound!

Whoso, desireless, have applied themselves
Firm-minded to the lore of Gotama,
They have won That which should indeed be won,
And having plunged into the Deathless State
Freely enjoy the Peace they have attained.
Yea, in the Order shines this glorious gem:
By virtue of this truth, may bliss abound!

Just as the firm post at the city gate
Doth stir not though the four winds on it blow,
So do I call him a good man and true
Who sees the Fourfold Ariyan Truth of things.
Yea, in the Order shines this glorious gem:
By virtue of this truth, may bliss abound!

Who clearly comprehends these Noble Truths
Well taught by Him of wisdom fathomless,
However heedless be they afterwards,
Into an eighth birth are not doomed to fall.
Yea, in the Order shines this glorious gem:
By virtue of this truth, may bliss abound!

As soon as he with insight is endowed
Three things become discarded utterly:
The lie of a perduring self, and doubt,
And clinging to vain rites and empty vows.
Escaped is he from the four evil states,
And of the six great sins incapable.
Yea, in the Order shines this glorious gem:
By virtue of this truth, may bliss abound!

Whatever evil deed in act or word,
Or even in his private thought he does,
Incapable is he of hiding it.
For such a thing (so hath it been declared)
He who has glimpsed the highest cannot do.
Yea, in the Order shines this glorious gem:
By virtue of this truth, may bliss abound!

Just as a forest grove puts forth its flowers
When the first month of summer heat doth come,
So, for the highest good of all, He preached
The Truth Sublime which to Nibbána leads.
Yea, in the Buddha shines this glorious gem:
By virtue of this truth, may bliss abound!

The Highest One, the Knower of the Highest,
The Giver and the Bringer of the Highest,
'Tis He Who taught the highest Truth of all.
Yea, in the Buddha shines this glorious gem:
By virtue of this truth, may bliss abound!

The old is withered out, the new becomes not;
Their minds desireth now no future birth.
Whoso have utterly destroyed the seeds
Of all existence, whose desires are quenched,
Extinguished are those wise ones as this lamp.
Yea, in the Order shines this glorious gem:
By virtue of this truth, may bliss abound!

Whatever beings are assembled here,
Creatures of earth or spirits of the sky,
To th' gods-and-men-adored Tathágata,
To th' Buddha, let us bow: may bliss abound!

Whatever beings are assembled here,
Creatures of earth or spirits of the sky,
To th' gods-and-men-adored Tathágata,
To th' Teaching, let us bow: may bliss abound!

Whatever beings are assembled here,
Creatures of earth or spirits of the sky,
To th' gods-and-men-adored Tathágata,
To th' Order, let us bow: may bliss abound!

OUTSIDE THE WALLS 1949

Tirokuddha Sutta

Outside the walls, at crossroads, do they stand,
And, to their homes returning, outside doors;
But when a meal of food and drink is spread,
A sumptuous meal, no man remembers them:
Such is the way of things. Wherefore it is
That in compassion for their kin deceased
Men make fit offerings at the proper time
Of food and drink, saying 'Be this a gift
Unto our kinsmen: may it gladden them.'
Then do those earth-bound kinsmen gather round
Where'er that feast of food and drink is spread,
Nor fail to render grateful thanks and say
'Long live our kinsman who hath made this gift!'
For there in ghostland is no herding seen,
Nor any ploughing of the fruitful fields;
There is no trading, as on earth there is,
Nor is there any trafficking with gold.
We, the departed spirits, there exist
On whatsoever things are offered here.
Even as water from the high ground flows
Down to the marshes lying at its foot,
So are the offerings that on earth are made
Of service to the spirits of the dead;
And as filled rivers flow to fill the sea,
So are the offerings that on earth are made
Of service to the spirits of the dead.
'Presents he made, did this and that for me;
They were my kinsmen, comrades, bosom-friends.'

Thus recollecting actions past, a man
Should give unto the ghosts in charity.
For of a truth, wailing and sorrowing
And many lamentations naught avail:
The ghosts are helped not when their kinsmen weep.
Besides, this alms unto the Order given
Will be of service for full many a day.
So is this duty to one's kinsmen told.
Unto the ghosts it is a gift of grace;
Unto the brethren of the Order, strength;
Unto yourselves, an ample merit won.

THE BURIED TREASURE   *1949*

Nidhikandha Sutta

In a deep hole beside some pond or stream
A man hides treasure, thinking in his heart,
'In time of need it will avail me much,
Or if perchance the king condemneth me,
If robber robs me, or to pay my debts,
Or else in time of famine, or when some
Mischance befalls me unexpectedly.'
Such in this world the weighty reasons are
For which a treasure is deposited.
But all this treasure cunningly concealed
In a deep hole beside some pond or stream,
It profiteth its owner not at all.
For either from its place it vanishes,
Or else his wits astray go wandering
And he remembers not its hiding-place,
Or else 'tis stolen by the serpent-gods,
Or goblins filch it from the secret place,
Or heirs unloved bear it by stealth away.
For when exhausted all one's merit is
That heap of treasure wholly perisheth.
But by much giving and by righteousness,
By self-control and taming of the self,
There is a precious treasure well concealed
For man or woman who will dig it up.
This is a treasure incommunicable,
Which thieves and robbers cannot steal away.
Let then the man of wisdom do good deeds:
This is the treasure that pursues a man.

This is that treasure which to gods and men
Bringeth all manner of delights. By this
The things they long for may in truth be won.
A fair complexion, a mellifluous voice,
Comely appearance, figure full of grace,
Power over men, and lengthy retinue,
This treasure can obtain them, every one.
Dominion and o'erlordship of the earth,
The bliss of wide-extended sovereignty
Dear to men's heart, yea, empery in heaven
Over the shining conclaves of the gods,
This treasure can obtain them, every one.
Prosperity on earth and joy in heaven,
The winning of the high Desireless State,
This treasure can obtain them, every one.
Whoso is blessed with goodly fellowship,
By efforts right wins knowledge and release
And self-control: all these are won thereby.
The Highest Wisdom, freedom of the mind,
The topmost summit of discipleship,
Illumination of the self by self,
Yea, ev'n the matchless state of Buddhahood,
This treasure can obtain them, every one.
Such power miraculous this treasure hath,
The treasure of good deeds: wherefore it is
Good deeds are done by wise and learned men.

SALUTATION TO THE THREE JEWELS   *1949*

Tiratana Vandana

To all the Awakened of the past,
To all the Awakened yet to be,
To all the Awakened that now are,
My worship flows unceasingly.
No other refuge than the Wake,
Refuge supreme, is there for me.
Oh by the virtue of this truth,
May grace abound, and victory!

To all Truth-teachings of the past,
To all Truth-teachings yet to be,
To all Truth-teachings that now are,
My worship flows unceasingly.
No other refuge but the Truth,
Refuge supreme, is there for me.
Oh by the virtue of this truth,
May grace abound, and victory!

To all the Brotherhoods that were,
To all the Brotherhoods to be,
To all the Brotherhoods that are,
My worship flows unceasingly.
No refuge but the Brotherhood,
Refuge supreme, is there for me.
Oh by the virtue of this truth,
May grace abound, and victory!

TRANSLATIONS FROM THE TIBETAN

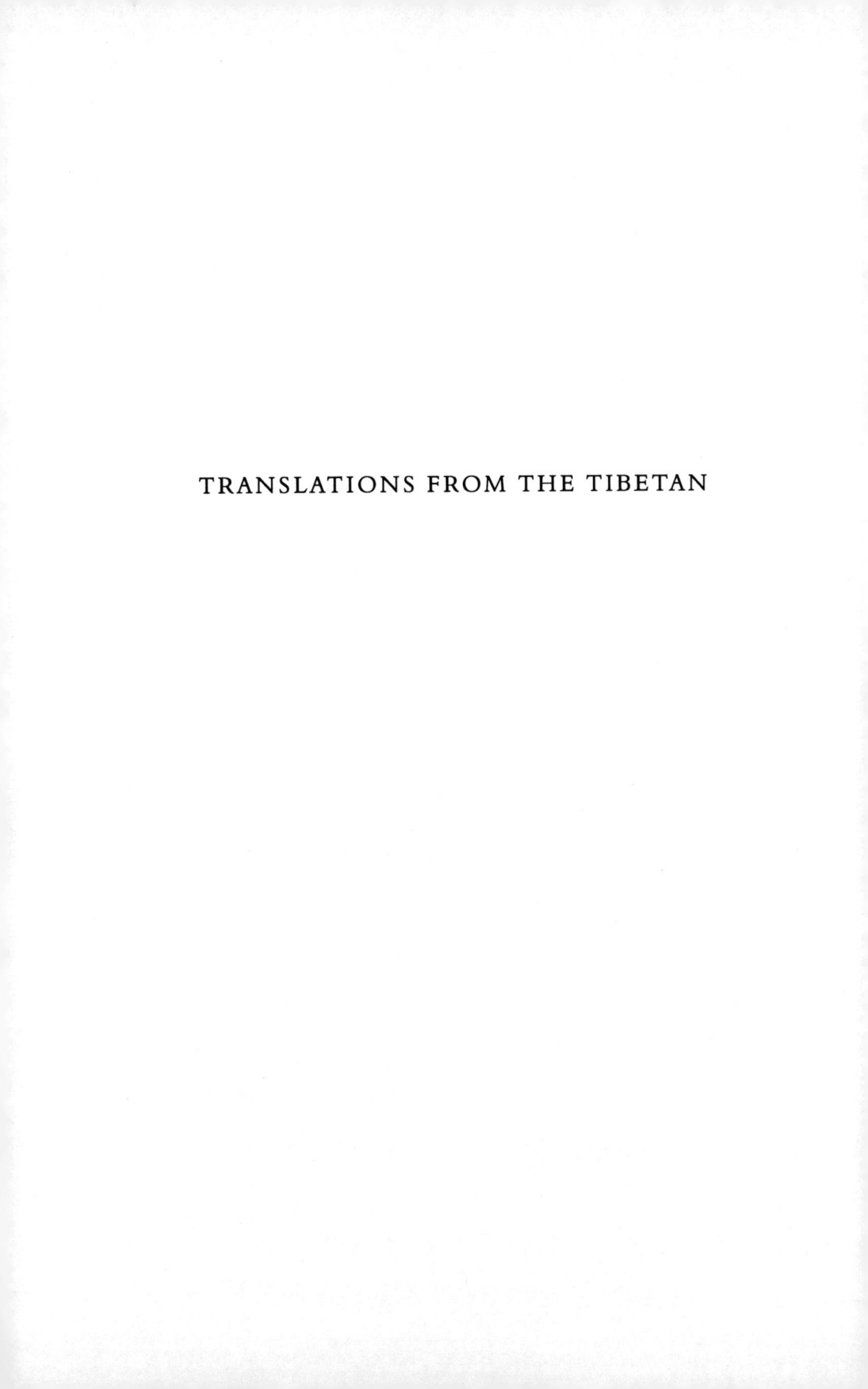

INVOCATION TO THE WRATHFUL DEITIES 1964

*From 'The Stream of the Immortality-Conferring Nectar
of the Esoteric Oral Tradition of the Lama's Bestowal of
the White Tara Abhishekha'
(Rendered according to the explanations of Ven. Dhardo Rimpoche)*

HUM
Burst forth, O Jnana blazing like fire at end of aeon!
Consume the blind darkness of delusion and craving,
And destroy all fear of the Yamaraja of hatred.
Great Heroes, recognizable by the tiger-skins (you are wearing),
Tramplers upon the hosts of Rakshasas and evil spirits, slayers of
    foes,
O Vidyarajas, O Wrathful Ones, be seated.
You are being summoned here to annihilate the evil spirits.
Puja is being performed for the benefit of all sentient beings:
Hence you must come.

HUM
Appearing from the non-duality of the Voidness and appearance,
You are ever devoted to the welfare of the world;
(You) having manifested yourselves with awe-inspiring body,
To you, O Greatly Wrathful Ones, I make obeisance.

Within, abiding in the peaceful Jnana,
Yet without of fearsome (foe-)devouring aspect,
Terribly roaring like a thousand claps of thunder,
And with these twain overcoming Rakshasas and demons,
To you, O Greatly Wrathful Ones, I make obeisance.

You whose essence is the highest Knowledge,
(Who) wielding in your hands all sorts of weapons
Have rooted out the kleshas and (deadly) poisons,
To you, O Snake-Adorned Ones, I make obeisance.

By fire like that at aeon's end encircled,
Hero-like you stand with flexed legs (wide) apart,
Angrily glaring with sun-and-moon-like eyeballs,
To you, O Consumer of the Yakshas, I make obeisance.

Greatly Fierce, like fire at end of aeon,
Splendid (white) tusks gleaming like a thousand lightning-flashes,
And shout like thousand thunder-claps forth sending,
To you, O Yaksha-killer, Wrathful King, I make obeisance.

HUM Roaring HUM and fear inspiring,
Yakshas destroying without exception,
Ye Gods, bestowers of all Siddhis whatsoever,
To you, Foes of the Yakshas, I make obeisance.

(Words in brackets represent explanatory additions by the translator.)

OFFERING THE MANDALA 1964

Meru, the king of mountains, on a ground
Of incense, sun and moon, the continents four,
I offer up to the Enlightened One,
Together with the Pure Land's radiant store.
O may all sentient beings, freed from pain,
The bliss of Full Enlightenment obtain!

Appendix I

INTRODUCTION TO 'THE VEIL OF STARS'

by Lama Anagarika Govinda

THE AUTHOR of this slender volume is a Buddhist monk who has already made a name for himself as a poet and writer. He has made the Himalayas his home.

The rhythm of the hills, the sparkling realms of the eternal snow above the clouds and the dark valleys in their shadow, the world of gods and the world of man, the realm of stars and the flowery meadows, have been the godfathers of these pearls of poetic thought and feeling. I call them pearls not only because they are precious and luminous, but because each of them forms a complete unit in itself, though in the way they are strung together they reveal a still deeper meaning, that goes beyond that of the single unit. And in this respect they are like all things in Nature, nay, like all living beings, who, in their subtle connection and relationship to each other as well as to the Infinite, are imbued with a transparent and transcendent quality beyond space and time, in love and death, in desire and renunciation, in joy and suffering. But it needs the sensitivity of the poet and the ecstasy of vision, that springs from a life of contemplation and inner awareness, to express it.

It was the poet in Sangharakshita that led him to the religious life, and it was the path of renunciation that enabled him to see the world in a wider and truer perspective, which is the hallmark of genuine poetry.

Here the words of Novalis come to one's mind:

> Poets and priests were one in the beginning, and only later times have separated them. The real poet, however, has always remained priest, just as the real priest has always remained poet.
>
> The poet is ever true. He remains constant in the cycle of Nature. The philosopher changes within the eternal immutability. The eternally immutable can only be represented by that which is changeable, the eternally changeable only in the immutable, the completeness of the present moment.

Each of Sangharakshita's poetic aphorisms is such a complete moment, in which the eternal presence is mirrored, and in which everybody will rediscover his or her own intimate experience; because poetry is the art of saying in simple words what the average man feels most profoundly, without being able to express it, and of putting into the language of feeling what the philosopher tries to express in terms of reason without ever being able to realize it. It is the art of giving meaning even to the inconspicuous, apparently trivial things of life, so that they stand out as something new and fresh, as if they had never been seen or felt before. This is the secret of spontaneous vision, the heart of creative meditation.

It was this attitude which made the Buddha 'see' the whole significance of illness, old age, and death, when he met (or had the 'vision' of) a sick man, an old man, and a corpse – sights which the ordinary person may meet a thousand times without being stirred, without experiencing anything, without realizing their significance.

It was this same attitude which, life after life, caused the Bodhisattva to sacrifice himself for others, and finally even to sacrifice his own personal liberation when it was within his reach at the time of Buddha Dipankara, and take upon himself the burden of innumerable rebirths and untold sufferings, in order to attain perfect enlightenment for the good of all, for the benefit of the whole world.

It is this Bodhisattva Ideal that inspires every line of this book and the life of its author. Infinite tenderness for all that lives begins as the love between two human beings, with all their faults and shortcomings, in which desire and possessiveness lead to infinite suffering and disillusionment. But these sufferings themselves are the purifying flame in which the limitations and impurities of that love are consumed, until a greater love emerges from the ordeal.

Thus pain and suffering are not something merely negative, something from which we should shrink or run away, but something that has to be faced and overcome in the battle of life, and which, for the sake of others, we should take upon ourselves unflinchingly, just as the Buddha did in his long career as a Bodhisattva. 'I wish to be bread for those who are hungry, drink for those who are thirsty,' exclaims Shantideva, who was as great a poet as he was a saint.

This ideal is nowadays conveniently forgotten by many of those who imagine themselves to be the keepers of the Buddha's word, though they have merely gone to sleep upon it, and who evade the real issues of life by sheltering behind cloistered walls and the armour of orthodoxy.

But a religion that is not strong enough to include the world, and love that is not great enough to go beyond the world, are not worthy of their name.

Love may or may not be bound up with desire, but it certainly cannot exist without an element of renunciation. Even what we call worldly love often proves stronger than life, stronger even than death. The greatest sacrifices that a human being is capable of, have been made for the sake of love. Because love means to give up something of ourselves, and perfect love means the complete surrender of our 'self'.

Therefore the very soil from which grows the renunciation of a Buddha, is the soil of love, in all its *human* forms. I emphasize the word *human*, because the Buddha's 'maitri' is not just a kind of cool or attenuated benevolence or well-meaning kindness; and his 'karuna' is not a kind of condescending compassion, but an attitude which is born out of the intense realization of oneness, in which there is no room for the difference of 'I' and 'thou', 'self' and 'other'.

Like a mother, whose love for her child flows naturally and without any trace of moral or spiritual superiority, simply from the feeling of an inseparable inner relationship and essential oneness, so the Buddha's 'maitri' and 'karuna' flow naturally from the all-embracing radiance of his mind and heart.

> The tear of the Bodhisattva's compassion flows through the world as love,
> Even as the austere snows of the Himalayas flow in rivers down into the green plains.

It is this spiritual background which gives to Sangharakshita's poetry its depth and emotional appeal. It rests on the inner parallelism between the most fundamental human emotions and the highest experiences on the path of liberation and enlightenment, the relationship between love and wisdom, the individual and the universal, the moods of Nature and the moods of the human heart. And this parallelism finds its expression in a juxtaposition of lines and a rhythmic flow of thoughts and words which can dispense with the outer embellishments of rhyme, because their inner relationship is strong enough to establish their harmony.

Sangharakshita's poetry reminds us of that of the Chinese Ch'an (Zen) School, in which this parallelism has been cultivated to the utmost perfection and simplicity, and in which the economy of words enhances their strength and significance. But this similarity is only natural. Sangharakshita's poetry flows from the same source and has grown into the same natural surroundings which inspired the Chinese Masters.

I cannot give any better illustration to characterize the form as well as the spirit of Sangharakshita's poetry than the following lines:

> Reality is reflected in my heart as love, and this love of mine is in turn mirrored in the all-embracing bosom of Reality,
> As though the moon lay reflected in the depths of the ocean, and the ocean in the calm clear heart of the moon.

Lama Anagarika Govinda
1954

Appendix II

ARGUMENT PREFIXED TO 'THE VEIL OF STARS'

THE LOVER is full of wonder at the coming of love, and feels that the transcendent beauty of the Beloved has opened for him a newer and higher world. Though ashamed to declare his love, he believes that the whole of Nature reveals it. But the Beloved shrinks from him, and in his despair the Lover feels that his passion has been frustrated. Yet it is impossible for him to forget the object of his adoration. He meets the Beloved every evening, but although a friendship does develop between them, it is not deep or close enough to satisfy the demands of the Lover, who is exasperated by the changeful moods of the Beloved and tortured by an outward proximity which only makes him feel more acutely their inner remoteness. Nevertheless he resolves to meet inconstancy with constancy, and increases his endeavours to win the Beloved's love. His mad pursuit brings him, however, no nearer to his goal, and his violent attempts to force a response from the Beloved meet only with rebuffs. In his despair he feels that even hatred would be preferable to such absolute indifference. All the joy of love now turns into pain. But from this pain he gradually learns of a higher love, and while reaffirming the eternity of his passion he resolves to accept the will of the Beloved in all things. A temporary separation teaches him that Love is above space no less than beyond time, and he begins to realize that it was the very impetuosity of his desire which had prevented its fulfilment. He begins to understand that spiritual Masters such as the Buddha deny satisfaction to desire, the lowest form of Love, only in order to grant it fulfilment in its highest form, Compassion. At this stage the Lover joyfully embraces the pain of Love, seeing in it a key not only to the mysteries of Art, but to the secrets of spiritual development. He retires for solace to the bosom of Nature, and under the influence of her peace purges his love of the dross of selfish desire. Yet far from imagining a duality between profane and sacred love, he sees that under the stress of experience desire naturally evolves into true Love, and Love into Compassion. Love destroys every thought of self, and the Lover feels the distinction of 'I' and 'Thou' fading away. Nothing in the universe is separate or independent, but as though in a mirror all reflect each, and each reflects all. With joy the Lover realizes that his own earthly love is only a faint reflection of the divine Compassion of the Bodhisattva. On the wings of this joy he rises to spiritual illumination, understanding the true nature of Love, and realizing that his own love, like all other things in the universe, is in turn reflected in the heart of Reality. Overflowing with gratitude to the Beloved for having revealed to him the Supreme Mystery of existence, he declares that after the recognition of the ultimate nature of Selfless Love there can be only Silence.

NOTES

1946. SYSTOLE AND DIASTOLE
Written after studying the writings of Arthur Avalon (Sir John Woodroffe) on the Hindu Tantra, as well as his translations of Sanskrit and Bengali Tantric texts.

1947. NIGHT THOUGHTS
Some of the imagery of the poem derives from Sinhalese classical poetry.

1949. TIRED OF THE CRIMSON CURTAIN...
Verse 5. The three worlds are the *kamaloka* or world of sensuous experience, the *rupaloka* or world of (archetypal) form, and the *arupaloka* or formless world; and the three bodies are the corresponding aspects/levels of our total (phenomenal) being, through which we have access to these worlds.

1950. MESSENGERS FROM TIBET
Verse 1. The asses were in fact mules.

1952. MANIFESTO
Verse 2. The emperor Ashoka (in the poem the name is a dysllable) inscribed his edicts on columns and rocks in many parts of India. In some of these he testifies to his faith in the Buddha and his teaching.

1953. NAGARJUNIKONDA
'The greatest Mahayana sage' is Nagarjuna. A Naga is a serpent or dragon, the Arjuna a kind of tree; hence 'dragon tree' in the last line of the poem.

1954. ELUSIVE BEAUTY
Verse 1. The poet is Baudelaire, who in his 'Hymne à la beauté' (*Les Fleurs du Mal* 22) asks 'Vien-tu du ciel profond ou sors-tu de l'abîme, / O Beauté?'

1955. KALINGA
Verse 1. The King is Ashoka, who on seeing the horrors wrought by his conquest of Kalinga abandoned violence for non-violence. 'Peacock tent' because the peacock was the emblem of the Maurya or Peacock Dynasty to which he belonged. I imagine the tent to have been emblazoned with peacocks or to have displayed a peacock banner.

1956. TO MANJUSHRI
Lines 8 and 9. 'Him whose keen mind could not brook / Impurity or error' refers to the Tibetan reformer Tsongkhapa.

1961. THE BUDDHA
Line 5. The 'blue-black elephants of heaven' are the storm-clouds. The image is traditional in Sanskrit poetry.

1961. TO SHRIMATI SOPHIA WADIA IN HONOUR OF HER SIXTIETH BIRTHDAY
Last verse. 48+60 = 108, which according to Indian tradition is an auspicious number.

1967. STANZAS
The line 'Hammer your thoughts into a unity' is a quotation from W.B. Yeats.

1967. POEMS FOR FOUR FRIENDS
2. To Miss———. Miss——— was Ven. Sochu Suzuki's charming young Japanese companion; hence 'a delicate touch of green' and 'the red blur of the rising sun'.

1975. SEQUENCE IN A STRANGE LAND
The strange land is Finland.

1975. THE BALLAD OF JOURNEYMAN DEATH
Prompted by a painting in the Academy Gallery, Helsinki.

1978. PADMALOKA
Verse 5. The poem was written on the eve of a visit to the Antipodes, where – from the standpoint of England – 'night is day, and day is night.'

1984. 6. THE LION OF ST MARK
Verse 3. The 'sumptuous pile' is the Doge's Palace and the 'three architectures' are (according to Ruskin) the Romanesque, the Gothic, and the Saracenic.

1986. THE BALLAD OF THE RETURN JOURNEY
'Toby' is the late T. Christmas Humphreys, Q.C., Founder-President of the Buddhist Society and judge of the High Court.

1992. WORK AND PLAY
The Sage of Weimar is Goethe. Helen and Euphorion (Byron) appear in *Faust*, Part Two.

1993. TO P——IN PRAGUE
The Defenestrations of Prague were the occasions when first the 'Protestant' Hussites (1419) and then the Catholics threw their opponents out of the windows of the Town Hall.

1994. THE POETRY OF FRIENDSHIP
Verse 5. The Fury is Atropos, the Fate who in Greek mythology cuts the thread of a man's life.

INDEX OF FIRST LINES

391 A golden flower held up, an answering smile –
367 A man was walking behind me
166 A solitary boy would sail his boat
262 A solitary figure, you pick your way
216 A sweet singing bird
261 A tangle of knotted branches on either side,
234 Above black pine-trees, on my homeward way,
 46 Above me broods
 41 Across the vastness of the sky
333 After the storm, the day dawns calm and fair,
200 After three months rain
354 Again with hideous thud the club descends,
213 Against a sky of purest turquoise rayed
130 All dreams of the soul
237 All living things should worship
167 All pleasures of all sense; the fickle mind's
310 Aloft on its tall stalk the sunflower hangs
 53 Aloft the many-petalled lotus rears
257 Alone in the fork
235 Along the tempting byways
103 Among all branched things, I for beauty choose
262 Among dense trees, dimly lit,
320 Among the mighty mountains sojourning,

255	Among the rich Autumn foliage
316	'An ineffectual angel', unable to do
109	As bellows roar, and red coals glow,
401	As children on a Summer's day
259	As the last gong-stroke dies away,
229	Asked 'What is Buddhism?' off they go,
262	At the wood's edge, a solitary hut;
23	Athens, the olive and grey eyes,
132	Autumn clouds, like snow
247	Away with prosy greetings!
233	Back to where the paths divided,
276	Bank holiday –
107	Because I could not muse apart
77	Before me through the evening air
351	Behind, ascending by degrees,
36	Behold the Clouded Dragon –
357	Behold the Lion of St Mark!
194	Believe not what you have heard
106	Below in the deep
232	Better, O Bull of Memphis, that we should
190	Between the mountain-crest and valley hung
341	Between the tree-clad hills the misty plain,
261	Beyond the deserted paddock, a dark wood;
334	Blake walked among the stones of fire,
377	Bowing I stand
127	Brain says, Beauty will perish,
84	Build thou upon thy spirit's mountainous height
318	By hope inspired, we make - though foiled
256	Careful! This morning
269	Cavern or shed, in the one-candled gloom
373	*Cheep cheep cheep* goes the sparrow,
205	Close, eyes; behold no more the rich array

95	Compassion is far more than emotion.
374	*Croak croak croak* goes the raven
387	Crystal ball, showing
312	Cut off from what I really think and feel,
133	Dawn brightening
340	Dear daughter of a tropic isle,
390	Defenestration was the word in Prague
212	Do we not love the dawn, when first
439	Dragons were slain here
200	Evening. Unstirred the western cloudlets lie
261	Façade after façade, along the Embankment,
93	Field-freshening rain,
313	Flanked by the lotus red
208	Flowers, that turn their faces to the sun,
338	Flýing slower, flýing faster,
232	For Poetry, this 'poem' shows,
266	For seven years a mask I wore,
124	For the Boundless, the Unlimited, the Infinite I long.
473	For welfare wishing, many gods and men
359	For years I bilked my debts, and bilked with mirth,
260	For you in the North, the first Winter snow;
384	For you the restless ocean,
126	Forgive me if I have stained
257	From a sky of unclouded
223	From pavilions of azure
265	From the ever-faithful Present
241	From the four compass-points a green, a gold,
256	From the train window
30	From the unlocked cage of my heart
214	From tone to tone of azure
382	Gods in the gallery I behold –
100	Golden in laughing sunlight,

331	Grasping the plough, with horse or ox they till
187	Grey sleepers, wrapped in noisome rags,
321	Half hoof-deep in the salt-encrusted sands
254	'Hammer your thoughts into a unity.'
81	Hardly in words these lips can tell
198	He could not find it with his wife and child,
353	He sits at ease upon the rocks,
228	He wanted that His followers should be flames
263	Heavy-winged, the last crow disappears
337	Her skin is greasy, and her garments stink.
92	Here on the river-brink I sit
31	Here perpetual incense burns;
195	Here, through the deep dark valley,
90	Here, where the Goatherd's banyan-tree
356	Heretics roasted for the love of Christ
324	High in the mountains, up creeks,
388	His dreams were visions. In the night
330	Horror and anguish! Madness and despair!
285	Hour after hour, day
243	How bare and dead the branch!
252	How beautiful is Berkeley Square!
87	How can I scorn the beggar's lot
182	How can wracked soul and ruined body pass
287	How did it feel
188	How like a bird it comes and goes,
132	How still the mists lie
114	How sweet is love's austerity,
43	How sweet it is, how sweet again
489	HUM / Burst forth, O Jnana…
301	I am the Windhorse!
299	I come to you with four gifts.
26	I did not seek, and so I found;

135	I feel like going on my knees
96	I have found you, India,
359	I laughed at death with women, wine, and song;
57	I listened all day for the knock of the Stranger,
227	I passed the square and scripted gate
128	I questioned, in my greener age,
134	I remember a pool of blue lotuses
61	I saw His shining footprints
110	I saw one misty morning
207	I saw two men, who nailed upon a cross
276	I should like to live
272	I should like to speak
146	I think there lives more wisdom
361	I walked across to the lecture hall,
264	I want to break out,
59	I will not read the scriptures
153	I'll write my poems for my friends,
218	If but the soil were richer
66	If thirst for truth doth like a fire
242	Impermanent, impermanent!
483	In a deep hole beside some pond or stream
344	In Amitabha's paradise, we're told,
117	In the dim green stillness of the pool
79	In the midnight of the dense ignorance of the world
94	In the saffron robe of yearning,
115	It is not love that seeks to bind
371	It was Lilith out of Eden,
34	It was the season after rain:
144	Knit with my heart these trumpets seem
375	*Kwark kwark* goes the eagle,
256	Last year the lightning
362	Late in your life you found the Eightfold Way,

306	Leafless, the walnut's twisting branches spread
244	Lean, strenuous, resolute, He passed His days
104	Let my life burn like incense
365	Living in Paradise
392	London Bridge is falling down,
49	Lord of the black locks, lord of thy handmaid,
203	Lord of the Lotus, Flaming Sword, and Book,
29	Lord, from my shadows do I flee
305	Los and Enitharmon wandered over the graves
129	Lost in these yellowing Autumn woods, I see
111	Love finds no fulfilment,
256	Lying on the bank
317	Manjushri sits upon his throne of gold,
122	Many were the friends who sought with eager hands
225	Men plucked like flowers which pass,
152	Men think that they have understood,
493	Meru, the king of mountains, on a ground
374	*Miao miao miao* goes the peacock,
327	*Mirror, mirror on the wall,*
125	Mock me not, O Rose, that I am hidden
206	More than ten years ago, old Father Thames,
98	Mountains bathed in mist
314	Moved by the spirit of the times, the heir
380	My friend has gone
335	My heart was held within an Angel's hands.
99	My heart-wick now is charred with sin,
387	My life is a dance
326	*My mind to me a kingdom is,*
319	My mind's a silver awning,
226	My soul between the feeling and the thought,
300	My Spectre stands there white as snow;
358	My wisdom cold? It was not cold

393	Myself into his book I hurled
284	Nightrace of silver-white coach of ghostly
161	*Natthi me saranam annam*
160	No fruit without the seed. Desire
352	Noblest of schools, the Royal today
161	Not where the gardens blossom;
175	Now he's gone, the best of squirrels,
149	Now it is early summer, and the woods
336	O Sacred Silence, now at last
150	Often do I remember the huge untidy nests
449	Often, now, I find myself
132	Oh darkness is done
176	Oh Death himself was Orpheus' audience!
339	Oh for a Persian garden,
298	'Oh what do you want, you wandering man,
240	Old frog on the brink
98	On the blue hill-side
133	On the hillside wait
256	On wind-tossed branches
311	Once more a virgin acolyte he stands
137	Once more the deep blue Winter skies
307	One by one the Gods
89	One need, and one need only,
379	One wears a yellow robe,
106	One white wave of snow
255	One would be far too many;
322	Osiris is green in colour, dark green.
201	Our heart's a shapeless clay-lump
74	Out of the sunset with the Evening Star,
481	Outside the walls, at crossroads, do they stand,
85	Outstretched upon the sandy ground
294	Páck your suitcase, cátch the train,

262	Paths left behind, I lose myself
217	Peach-bloom, each Springtide, fills my heart with grief
386	People like things labelled. They want to know
274	Petals
369	Pine-scent is a great thing,
459	Pink and white upon the hillside
393	Read aloud,
211	Reading some books, you'd think the Buddha-Way,
172	Red as roses blushing,
181	Red-bannered hatred fills the streets
32	Roll forth, O Conquering Wheel,
121	Roll on, roll on for ever,
180	Round this boundless universe's
295	Rusty pine-needles
91	Seeing this world, this hapless world,
344	Seek not in gloomy charnel-grounds to see
389	Seen through the fanlight
148	Selling wild orchids at my door one day
359	Short were my steps upon the earth, and few,
67	Since that auspicious Full-Moon Day
173	Since that his eyes were like two wells
387	Sing? This is not the time for singing.
360	So love grew up between us like a flower,
141	Some men can find no word for Love:
290	Space, infinite space! Heather
224	Spring, in my boyhood it was understood,
342	St Francis in the Umbrian glades
372	Stand still, O Time, that I may see,
268	Suddenly he was there. The darkness glowed
145	Sun, moon, the mountains and the plain,
344	Sunk in the stream-bed where the hills begin
394	Surely king Mark was mad,

55	Swanlike, upon the Sun-Path let me soar
260	Taking a sudden turn, the sunlit path
289	Talkative one morning, the Cypriot barber
258	Tenderly smiling, White Tara
130	That is all very well…
113	The ashes of all my heartaches,
261	The candle has long since guttered and died,
417	The coming of love is mysterious as the flight of a bird
47	The dim sun sinks to rest
291	'The early Christians
105	The gardener crops his rose-tree's hundred buds,
328	The gods, throned in their radiant overworld,
220	The hills of the horizon
165	The icy wind has planted
330	The lion, the horse, the elephant, the whale;
154	The loose red earth is washed away,
88	The Lotus blooms tonight,
164	The moon is cold and hard and small
251	The morning sunshine saturates the heavenly blue
257	The multitudinous whisper
33	The noise of day is hushed at last,
364	The oak stands in the forest
368	The past is in the mind,
363	The people of Bethnal Green are not beautiful,
240	The periwinkle flowers among the stones,
332	The poet is the world's interpreter,
395	The poetry of friendship
246	The politician on the platform
250	The quick sap rises in the dry stalk;
155	The rain has been falling all day;
243	The red leaf falls upon the lake below.
147	The red rose does not whisper

255	The small blue monkey
186	The stream of my desire no more
159	The surest way of gaining is to give.
54	The swiftest, sweetest pen could ne'er indite
222	The Teesta in the Summer
196	The third day of the slaughter saw a change;
177	The thunders rolled beneath me, as I sate
283	The time has come
328	The Tree! the Tree! the Wish-fulfilling Tree!
170	The wisest doubt if Truth
112	The world is full of falling leaves,
234	These gods and goddesses that men have framed,
286	They are decidedly
315	They sing with fairest looks and sweetest breath,
28	Thine is the outward action,
202	Think not, my friends, that piling stone on stone,
255	This bright Autumn morning
475	This must be done by one who kens his good,
48	Those who have hid themselves on heights of snow,
72	Thou art not dead, nor dost Thou even sleep
221	Though depths of perfect azure
292	Though one's food is not perfect
119	Though rained thy kisses on His hand
230	Though sinks into the western hills
136	Though veil on veil of gleaming blue
243	Though vigorously the high wind shakes the bough,
267	Three nails were enough for your Lord. But you
308	Three Summers and three Autumns have I seen,
282	Three weeks before he died
345	Three years in earth had Johnson slept,
323	Thrown on the white wall
63	Tired of the crimson curtain,

304	'Tis Chaucer's month, the merry month
485	To all the Awakened of the past,
199	To Him Who on that night of sleeping flowers
257	To stand naked
278	Tonight at noon
277	Too long have I been a camel
131	Tread softly as a cat
373	*Trill trill trill* goes the blackbird
80	Truth is not truth, unless to men it is
375	*Tu-whit tu-whoo* goes the owl,
65	Turn away from the world, weary pilgrim,
236	Twisting, writhing, leaping,
143	Up and down the gravel path,
240	Visitors all day!
142	Walking along the mountain paths,
27	Water from the thawed-out snow
151	Waterfalls from stone
171	We cannot sing as Orpheus wist
58	We cry that we are weak although
139	We know when market-day is near,
116	We walked where thick green bamboo groves
193	We who have seen men murdered,
191	Well might the Poet question
120	What a fantastic creature is the poet,
366	What agonies await him now,
349	What can it do, when friends avert
325	What said you, *Short, swift swallow-flights of song?*
217	What though so near upon the tree
219	What though the mining's done, th' ore told?
230	What though with cloud the sky be grey,
38	What thoughts are present to Thy mind
178	What will you say to those

477	Whatever beings are assembled here,
24	Whén the latency of thought
209	When Inspiration cracks the moulds of verse
40	When Truth and Good like phantoms fade
101	Whence come these asses, brazen-belled,
44	Where green and purple strips of earth
183	Where hills humped, there must be
157	Where the ice glitters, where untrodden snows
174	Whether within his mind dark forces rolled
151	White clouds on the hills
108	White mist drifts down the valley dim,
257	White-winged for an instant
329	With barrel-bellies, mouths like needle-eyes,
189	With grey-green fir and blue-black pine communing,
215	With kingcups from the meadow
355	With looks demure, and tress that down her cheek
118	With slender rosy stem
239	With sweet compassionate faces,
62	'With your holy vows,
385	Within the shadowy colonnade
238	Wonder it is to dwell at last
383	'Work is the companion,'
210	Work out the secret of your blood. The bright
253	Yellow in green, by woods we chance to pass,
197	Yet shall my soul burn upward like a fire.
280	You are the distance
231	You remind me of whatever's made of gold –
245	You were my mother once, the Scriptures say,
270	You wrote four letters, one
185	Your beauty, in repose, is like a vase
204	Your sadness is my sadness, friend, and so

The Windhorse symbolizes the energy of the Enlightened mind carrying the Three Jewels – the Buddha, the Dharma, and the Sangha – to all sentient beings.

Buddhism is one of the fastest growing spiritual traditions in the Western world. Throughout its 2,500-year history, it has always succeeded in adapting its mode of expression to suit whatever culture it has encountered.

Windhorse Publications aims to continue this tradition as Buddhism comes to the West. Today's Westerners are heirs to the entire Buddhist tradition, free to draw instruction and inspiration from all the many schools and branches. Windhorse publishes works by authors who not only understand the Buddhist tradition but are also familiar with Western culture and the Western mind.

For orders and catalogues contact

WINDHORSE PUBLICATIONS
UNIT 1-316 THE CUSTARD FACTORY
GIBB STREET
BIRMINGHAM
B9 4AA
UK

WINDHORSE PUBLICATIONS (USA)
14 HEARTWOOD CIRCLE
NEWMARKET
NEW HAMPSHIRE
NH 03857
USA

ALSO FROM WINDHORSE

SANGHARAKSHITA
THE RELIGION OF ART

Just as beauty is truth, and truth beauty, the spiritual life and the artistic life are inextricably linked.

A work of art not only expresses its creator's clearest insight and most refined emotion, it also acts as a means through which we may experience something of the beauty he has perceived. Properly approached, both religion and art lead to an expansion of consciousness, a state of heightened awareness and understanding in which, ultimately, the limiting boundaries of 'self' no longer hold.

In this collection of essays, Sangharakshita offers a manifesto for a radical appraisal of art and religion.

172 pages
ISBN 0 904766 31 4
Paperback £5.99/$11.95

SANGHARAKSHITA
FACING MOUNT KANCHENJUNGA

In 1950 Kalimpong was a lively trading town in the corner of the world where India runs into Nepal, Bhutan, Sikkim, and Tibet. Like a magnet, it attracted a bewildering array of guests and settlers: ex-colonials, Christian missionaries, princes in exile, pioneer Buddhologists, incarnate lamas from the Land of Snows – and Sangharakshita, the young English monk who was trying to establish a Buddhist movement for local youngsters.

In a delightful volume of memoirs, glowing with affection and humour, the author shares the incidents, encounters, and insights of his early years in Kalimpong. These include a brush with the Bombay film industry, a tour with the relics of the Buddha's chief disciples, a meeting with Dr B.R. Ambedkar, a friendship with Lama Anagarika Govinda, and much more.

Behind the events we witness the transformation of a rather eccentric young man into a unique and confident individual, completely at home in his adopted world, and increasingly effective as an interpreter of Buddhism for a new age.

512 pages
ISBN 0 904766 52 7
Paperback £11.95/$24.00